PRAISE FOR

LEADING THE WAY

"At last, a book on how to grow leaders throughout the organization that penetrates the clichés and simple-minded formulas to reveal the requisite embedded web of attitudes and practices. Grounded in talent-building organizations that are also successful financially, the authors manage to be both clear and subtle—just as great leaders must be—and deliver practical, thought-provoking ideas. Our futures depend on these ideas spreading."

> Allan R. Cohen, Edward A. Madden Distinguished Professor of
> Global Leadership, Babson College
> Coauthor, *Power Up: Transforming Organizations
> Through Shared Leadership*

"Most companies now understand that having better leaders pays off enormously, and *Leading the Way* shows how to get those leaders from inside."

> Peter Cappelli, George W. Taylor Professor of Management,
> Director, Center for Human Resources,
> The Wharton School, University of Pennsylvania

"*Leading the Way* is inspiring from the start, emphasizing what IBM has long believed: People are our greatest asset, and investing in their leadership and talent is critical to the future success of the company. This book is an essential read for all leaders."

> Donna Riley, Vice President, Global Talent, IBM

"Selecting and developing leaders is the lifeblood of any organization. By creating a learning environment where leaders are challenged and constantly refining their skills, an organization builds bench strength for sustainability. Gandossy and Effron identify the qualities that constitute a true learning environment and share ideas from top organizations where there is a genuine investment in leadership development."

Dennis M. Donovan, Executive Vice President
Human Resources, The Home Depot

"The demands for growth emphasize leadership like never before. Gandossy and Effron present a compelling case and a clear roadmap for building these leaders in your company!"

Michael Treacy, author, *Double-Digit Growth,*
and Chief Strategist, GEN3 Partners

"In a field crowded with opinion books and unsubstantiated thinking, *Leading the Way* is a gem about how to produce the leadership talent companies need in the 21st century. Lucid, comprehensive, and based on groundbreaking research, it enables us to clearly understand why some organizations succeed and others fall behind."

Andrew Sobel, author, *Making Rain* and *Clients for Life*

"In all the years I've been consulting on leadership, one constant struggle has been determining what factors make one organization's leadership programs and practices better than the next. *Leading the Way* . . . explores that issue head-on and provides compelling and practical answers. The authors give insight into both the big and little things that make the difference. Every leader will gain immensely from the ideas put forth in this book."

Jack Zenger, coauthor of *The Extraordinary Leader*
and Vice Chairman of Novations Group

"This book is a refreshing antidote to the hand-wringing headlines and board laments over the presumed leadership shortage. *Leading the Way* gives fresh, behind the scenes practical insights into just how this leadership building is really done—saving top executives and HR professionals from expensive, time consuming benchmarking trips and misleading PR spin. Gandossy and Effron uniquely examine top echelon HR practices and leadership development against strategic purpose, company culture, and corporate performance."

Professor Jeffrey Sonnenfeld,
Associate Dean, Yale School of Management

Leading the Way

Leading the Way

Three Truths from the Top Companies for Leaders

Robert Gandossy and Marc Effron, Hewitt Associates

WILEY

JOHN WILEY & SONS, INC.

Published by John Wiley & Sons, Inc., Hoboken, New Jersey.
Published simultaneously in Canada.

For general information on our other products and services please contact our Customer Care Department within the United States at (800) 762-2974, outside the United States at (317) 572-3993 or fax (317) 572-4002.

Wiley also publishes its books in a variety of electronic formats. Some content that appears in print may not be available in electronic books. For more information about Wiley products, visit our web site at www.Wiley.com.

Library of Congress Cataloging-in-Publication Data:
Gandossy, Robert P.
  Leading the way : three truths from the top companies for leaders / Robert Gandossy and Marc Effron.
    p. cm.
  Includes bibliographical references and index.
  ISBN 0-471-48301-X (cloth)
  1. Leadership. 2. Executive ability. 3. Chief executive officers. 4. Boards of directors.
  5. Management. I. Effron, Marc. II. Title.
  HD57.7.G36 2004
  658.4′092—dc22

                                                                    2003015166

Printed in the United States of America
10 9 8 7 6 5 4 3 2 1

CONTENTS

Foreword   ix

Acknowledgments   xv

About the Authors   xix

Chapter 1
The Looming Leadership Crisis   1

Chapter 2
Leadership Truth #1: CEOs and Boards of Directors
at Top Companies Provide Leadership and Inspiration   25

Chapter 3
Leadership Truth #2: Top Companies Have a Maniacal Focus
on the Best Talent   49

Chapter 4
Leadership Truth #3: Top Companies Put in Place the Right
Programs, Done Right   73

Chapter 5
Pay Attention to Subtlety: The Little Things Are the
Big Things   113

Chapter 6
Starting from Scratch to Build a Strong Leadership
Pipeline   131

Chapter 7
Future Directions: New Rules for the 21st Century   157

Epilogue   179

Appendix A
Top 20 Companies for Leaders List, 2002 and 2003   181

Appendix B
Building a Company of Great Leaders: A Starter Kit   183

Index   213

FOREWORD

There is a huge difference between two apparently similar words—
"simple" and "easy." While the insights from *Leading the Way* may
seem simple to understand, they are far from easy to execute. If everything in this book is common sense (which I believe it is), then
why are so few companies *implementing* these practices?

I had been in the leadership development business for 12 years before anyone asked me the great question: *Do any of the leaders who participate in these programs ever* really *change?* Having a background in
mathematics, I gave a candid response. My honest, yet embarrassed,
reply was, "I don't know."

For the past 15 years, I have been uncovering the answer to this
question. What have I learned? *Can* leaders change? Definitely! *Will*
leaders change? Maybe.

Historically, there has been little real research to indicate that leadership development has made a positive, long-term difference. There
has been almost no documentation that leaders changed or that organizations became more effective. At the end of traditional training
programs, participants evaluated the external and internal faculty.
They evaluated the human resources (HR) department. They even
evaluated the quality of the hotel rooms and the food. While this approach may have produced clever consultants, dedicated HR staff
members, clean rooms, and good food, there is little hard evidence
that it helped produce great leaders!

Leading the Way breaks this cycle by presenting compelling,
groundbreaking research that proves that the investment in develop-

ing leaders delivers superior long-term financial results. From detailed data gathered from more than 600 companies around the world, including hundreds of interviews with line executives and human resource leaders, Bob Gandossy and Marc Effron extracted the three foundation elements, or Truths, that are the foundation for all Top Companies for Leaders.

- Chief Executive Officers (CEOs) and boards of directors at Top Companies provide leadership and inspiration.
- Top Companies have a maniacal focus on the best talent.
- Top Companies put in place the right programs, done right.

These three leadership Truths exist at all of the Top 20 Companies for Leaders, and they provide clear direction to companies wanting to increase the quality and depth of their leaders. I suspect that none of the Top Companies would tell you that what they did was easy. They might not even say it was simple, and to do this while consistently delivering strong financial results was tougher still.

Implementing the practices described in this book requires *courage*. For example, "Leadership and inspiration from the CEO and board" is a key practice that is recommended in this book. That sounds simple enough. In fact, asking CEOs and board members to be inspiring and demonstrate leadership in building their company's leaders seems like it should hardly be necessary! Real executive involvement takes courage. In the first chapter, you'll read how Lou Gerstner had the courage to stand up to his management team and insist that they "go back to school." He had the courage to stand behind the direction of the new IBM. His attitude was "let's take the responsibility to make it work," not "let's sit back and evaluate to see if it might work."

Involvement from the CEO often takes courage on the part of

leadership development staff members. It can be a lot easier to brief CEOs on leadership development than to have them get involved. If CEOs get involved, they may not like what they see. They may get annoyed. This may even be career-threatening to the leadership development staff!

It takes courage to involve the board in this process. The less courageous CEO might consider board involvement as meddling or playing on his or her turf. The courageous CEO knows that board members who care about building leadership quality, want to get to know the company's high-potential leaders, and show proper oversight of the executive team's actions, make the company a stronger place that provides a better experience for leaders and shareholders alike. The boards at companies like PepsiCo, The Home Depot, and General Electric (GE), all of whom are actively involved in building leaders, serve as great examples of courage in action.

A maniacal focus on top talent sounds simple. Just figure out who the highest-potential leaders are, let them know they are high-potentials and work especially hard to help them develop. This takes courage. Many companies develop their best talent through frequent developmental moves that, if done right, benefit both the organization and the leader. Less courageous companies make the safe move by putting leaders in place who can easily perform the role. Courageous companies stretch their leaders in assignments where the very potential risk of failure causes greater effort and accelerated learning.

Executives have to show the courage to make the hard decisions about who is on the list and who isn't. Many people may get angry or upset. Some may even leave the company. Executives will invariably make a few *wrong* decisions. They run the risk of looking stupid in public when they make the wrong choices. For years, many companies have kept their lists of high-potential leaders a secret to avoid conflict and confrontation.

One of my clients is one of the world's largest professional-services firms. When they studied turnover they discovered that half of the professionals who were leaving the firm were people who were going to be promoted to partner. Almost all would have stayed if they had only known that they were considered special and important. The firm finally realized that the risk involved in alienating the bottom half of performers was not as great as the risk associated with losing the top 10 percent.

The Right Programs, Done Right Truth sounds simple enough. Human resource groups should make sure their leadership programs tightly link to the behaviors they say are important, avoid having any leadership process becoming bureaucratic, and measure the effectiveness of what they're doing on a regular basis. This sounds like the simplest request of all, but *Leading the Way* shows that very few firms do all of these activities. All of them take courage.

Linking leadership programs means taking a clear stance on what is—and what isn't—important to the company. It means taking the chance of making a wrong decision. It might even mean admitting that some of what you currently do, you shouldn't do in the future. *Avoiding bureaucracy* means challenging yourselves to serve your customers in new ways, to understand what they consider to be the ideal experience, by eliminating activities in which the line finds no value. *Measuring effectiveness* means actually evaluating whether programs are making a real difference. It means taking the chance of actually proving that something didn't work. It's done regularly at the Top Companies, but rarely at the other companies that Hewitt surveyed and interviewed.

Leading the Way shows *courage* by rejecting the best practice framework that offers easy answers to tough leadership challenges. Building leaders is not easy; the path looks different at each company, but drawing inspiration from others, not blindly copying them, will bring the best results. I believe that the companies that do it best in developing leaders have one thing in common. They have courage.

As you read this book, challenge yourself. Realize that all of the seemingly simple suggestions are actually far from easy. Have the courage to learn from the best and be willing to take the risk to do what is right.

—Marshall Goldsmith

Acknowledgments

This book has many voices. It has the voice of leaders at Top Companies who told about their formative years, the events and people who influenced them, and their role as leaders. It has the voice of human resource professionals who patiently explained the processes they have in place to build great leaders. And this book has the voices of our clients—those who struggle with the everyday challenge of building companies where great talent thrives. We thank all for their stories, their ideas, and their inspiration.

We'd like to thank executives at Centex, Colgate-Palmolive, Federal Express, General Electric, The Home Depot, Honeywell International, IBM, Intel, PepsiCo, Pfizer, Procter & Gamble, Southwest Airlines, and SYSCO for their help and insights.

Many leaders at Top Companies provided special insights, help, and support. We'd especially like to thank the following: Larry Hirsch and Bob Stewart at Centex; Coleen Smith and Bob Joy at Colgate-Palmolive; Dave Bronczek of FedEx Express, and Larry MacMahan formerly of FedEx; Lucien Alziari of PepsiCo; Susan Peters at GE; Randy MacDonald, Donna Riley, and Obed Louissant at IBM; David Cote and Tom Weidenkopf at Honeywell International; Procter & Gamble's A. G. Lafley and Dick Antoine; Bob Nardelli, Dennis Donovan, and their teams at The Home Depot; and the countless others who gave us their time.

This book, too, has the voice of others we have learned from over the years—those whose writings, research, and wise counsel have influenced our thinking and perspective. There are many such influences: Rosabeth Moss Kanter, Jeff Pfeffer, Marshall Goldsmith, Morgan McCall, Jr., Dave Ulrich, Noel Tichy, and Warren Bennis have profoundly influenced the way we think about organizations and the leaders who lead them. Their influence can be seen, too, in the Top Companies.

Like the Top Companies, Hewitt has its own top talent and leadership who were invaluable to us. The list is long, but must begin with Lauren Cantlon Tate. Lauren helped conduct most of the interviews, analyzed data, conducted follow-ups, researched, checked, rechecked, edited, and reedited. She's both wise and special beyond her years. We can't thank her enough.

Shelli Greenslade and Pi Wen Looi conducted much of the research and analyses for the Top Companies study. Karen Barnes, Andrew Bell, Bob Campbell, Tom Hauser, Richard Kantor, Lisa Labat, Phil Murray, and Andrea Riccioni are colleagues whom we value and whose ideas and insights are reflected on these pages. Don Minner, Joe Micucci, and Kyra Ramsey were helpful, supportive, and importantly, enthusiastic about this project. We thank all of you for your friendship and help.

And then there is Julie Offord. You wouldn't be reading these pages were it not for Julie. She, too, is special. Julie was a master at keeping schedules and making sure things stayed on track, while consistently maintaining the quality. And she makes us laugh. We thank you.

Most of the royalties from this book will be donated to charities that are committed to the growth and development of leaders of diverse backgrounds. We will donate royalties to two charities: The Drucker Foundation and the Minority Pipeline Alliance. We thank you for the strong moral direction your organizations provide to so many.

We'd also like to thank Matt Holt and his team at John Wiley &

Sons. Matt was both supportive and enthusiastic about this project from the start, and we thank him for his guidance.

RPG
ME

This was fun to do. But I'm fairly certain it wasn't fun all the time for those closest to me—Taylor, Dylan, Connor, and Simone. They had to endure hours of stories, a crazy schedule, and disruption to our normal life, if there is such a thing in a family with three teenagers. I thank you for your patience and your love. A special thanks goes to Taylor for taking out the red pen, editing every page, and providing a little payback for all the years Dad did that to her. Thanks. Finally, Simone: editor, advisor, supporter, mother, and wife. No one could ask for a better partner in life.

RPG

To Michelle for your love and inspiration; Madison (the cat) for your company on the 10 P.M.–1 A.M. writing shift; Andrea Riccioni, Lisa Labat, and the leadership team for partnering with me to build this practice; my clients for the honor of learning from you; Bob Campbell for telling me "you can always come back"; and Marshall Goldsmith for helping me to "let it go" (well, most of it!). Thank you all.

ME

ABOUT THE AUTHORS

Robert Gandossy
Bob is a Global Leader for Hewitt Associates' Talent and Organization Consulting. He has special expertise in improving organizational effectiveness, human resource strategy, leadership, managing large-scale change, mergers and acquisitions, and increasing growth through innovation.

He has written articles and books on a variety of subjects, including human-resource strategy, mergers and acquisitions, change management, innovation, and business ethics. He was a co–project manager of a major research effort, *The Changing American Workforce in the 1980s,* and his book *Bad Business* was called a "masterful job" by Tom Peters and "high drama and a fascinating story" by Rosabeth Moss Kanter. He is the coeditor (with Marc Effron and Marshall Goldsmith) of the book *Human Resources in the 21st Century* (John Wiley & Sons, April 2003), featuring chapters by the world's thought leaders in the fields of leadership and human resources. He is the coeditor (with Jeff Sonnenfeld) of a forthcoming book on *Leadership and Governance* (2004).

Bob has been a speaker for a number of groups, including Harvard Business School, Human Resources Planning Society, The Wharton School, Tom Peters Group, Yale Law School, Yale's School of Organization and Management, World At Work, American Management Association, and The Conference Board. He has spoken to audiences in cities all over the world, including Hong Kong, Singapore, Shanghai, New Delhi, Paris, London, and Brussels.

Bob holds a B.S. degree from Harpur College and a Ph.D. from Yale University, where he specialized in the study of organizational behavior.

Marc Effron

Marc is the Global Practice Leader for Hewitt Associates' Leadership Consulting Practice. He works with the world's leading corporations to help them build the quality and depth of their leaders. His work focuses on developing corporate leadership strategies, building executive team succession management processes, and assessing and coaching senior leaders.

Marc guides Hewitt's research efforts on leadership—creating and now managing Hewitt's Top Companies for Leaders global research. The findings are featured as a cover story each year in *Chief Executive* magazine. He is also coeditor, with Robert Gandossy and Marshall Goldsmith, of *Human Resources in the 21st Century,* and is author of articles that appear in *The Change Champions Field Guide* and *Ideas on the Move.*

Marc's prior experience includes serving as senior vice president of leadership development for Bank of America, as director of organization effectiveness and learning for Oxford Health Plans, and as a compensation consultant for a global consulting firm in New York. He previously served as a political consultant and a congressional staff assistant.

Marc has spoken to business groups and conferences throughout the world. He is widely quoted on leadership issues, including in recent articles in the *The New York Times, Asian Wall Street Journal, European Wall Street Journal, HR Executive, Financial Times,* and others.

He earned a BA degree in Political Science from the University of Washington and an MBA with honors letters from the Yale School of Management. He is based in Hewitt's northeast regional headquarters in Norwalk, Connecticut.

CHAPTER 1

THE LOOMING LEADERSHIP CRISIS

Leaders aren't born, they are made. And they are made just like anything else, through hard work.

—Vince Lombardi

SURVEYING THE crowd at the first meeting of IBM's Senior Leadership Group in 1996, Lou Gerstner, the blunt-talking chief executive charged with saving Big Blue from the brink, issued an edict: Go back to school! The directive must have surprised and likely angered more than a few of the 300 senior executives—including Gerstner's own direct reports—many of whom had been with the tech giant for decades.

But Gerstner hadn't been recruited from R. J. R. Nabisco to make friends. His immediate challenge was to save an institution that had quite literally been placed on a 24-hour deathwatch. Those in the room that day understood they had been hand selected because they were critical to IBM's recovery. So, when Gerstner told them they would be participating in a program focused on developing their own leadership capabilities, they knew they'd better listen.

That's not to say that everyone had confidence in Gerstner's ability to breathe new life into IBM. A downward spiral had taken the company's $6 billion profit in 1990 and quickly turned it into an $8.1 billion loss by 1993. In an industry that was rapidly expanding, IBM had lost half of its market share since 1985. They ranked 11th in customer satisfaction among companies in the computer industry, trailing several companies that no longer existed. IBM's stock price stood at an all-time low, and competitors like Hewlett-Packard and EMC clawed at its market share. On April 1, 1993, the day Gerstner took charge, IBM's stock had dropped from a high of $43 per share in 1987 to $13 per share.

The organization that had long held court as America's most admired company was forced to abandon its practice of lifetime employment, sending tens of thousands of workers in search of new jobs. Many of those workers found employment within the legions of new dot.coms and undoubtedly snickered at IBM as a soon-to-be-extinct dinosaur. However, it wouldn't be the dot.com millionaires but Big Blue that would ultimately have the last laugh.

Just as Wall Street was preparing to throw the first shovelful of dirt onto IBM's casket, something miraculous happened: The giant rose from the dead. In 2001, profits reached over $8 billion on revenues of $83 billion, and shares hit an all-time high. The company once credited by The Washington Post for inventing the computer industry was back—with a vengeance. And, in an instance of ultimate irony, BusinessWeek declared IBM the largest dot.com in the world. Gerstner and his team had pulled off the turnaround of the century, leading IBM back to profitability—without chopping the company into separate operating units, a plan that had been in the works when he took over as chief executive.

While Gerstner himself has been given much of the credit for IBM's amazing turnaround, Big Blue's boss clearly recognized that the company's leadership strength extended far beyond his office.

On his watch, a comprehensive approach to building great leaders was crafted, including careful selection, development, and rewards for IBM's best talent. Leaders were held accountable for growing other leaders, and good leadership was viewed as a critical asset to be carefully managed for the best possible return.

Gerstner's mandate accomplished much more than saving IBM. It posi-

tioned the company for the future by building a deep bench to ensure that Big Blue's dramatic turnaround wasn't just a passing phase. The fact that the transition from Gerstner to new CEO Sam Palmisano in 2002 was flawless in the eyes of the hypersensitive stock market and critical business press drives that point home. And with IBM facing likely retirement of as much as 75 percent of its senior management team by the year 2007, Gerstner's investment in a powerful leadership-development and succession-management process will prove to be an absolute necessity if IBM is to retain its regained crown and Gerstner's turnaround legacy is to last.

REACHING THE BOILING POINT

As Gerstner's story demonstrates, it is the development of a strong leadership team, rather than the actions of a single individual, that sets one organization apart from the rest. The facts are indisputable: Great leadership teams build trust and confidence among their people. They motivate and inspire. They anticipate challenges and redirect the enterprise in timely and appropriate ways, unifying the workforce behind a single cause and driving the kind of performance that allowed a Southwest Airlines to soar or an IBM to reboot itself. Simply put, they deliver better business results, and the opposite is true as well: An incompetent leadership team wreaks serious damage and creates inflexible bureaucracies, often destroying shareholder value and dooming the organization to failure. The corporate landscape is littered with hundreds of overly managed, poorly led institutions.

Tales of leadership successes and failures have served as juicy fodder for the likes of *The Wall Street Journal,* CNN, and Fox News. They've put leadership on the map, awakening many sleeping corporate giants in the process. It's clear now that there is a cause and effect—great returns for those organizations that invest in leaders and

failure for those that do not. After decades of largely paying lip service to building great leaders, executives everywhere have begun to
think more seriously about their own leadership processes.

This new awareness arrives at the right moment as two daunting
demographic trends loom. Those trends will forcefully challenge how
companies develop their leadership talent. In the 1970s, 1980s, and
1990s, companies became spoiled by the enormous baby boomer
generation—the pig moving through the python—which provided
millions of talented, dedicated workers. While efforts were made to
increase the capabilities of this group, the mindset that you could
"buy" a leader when needed became ingrained in many firms. Revenue at executive-search firms nearly tripled in the seven-year period from 1993 to 2000 as companies tried to find outside what they
could not or did not develop inside.[1] "Twenty years ago," says Jeff
Sonnenfeld, associate dean at Yale's School of Organization and
Management, "only 7 percent of major firms hired CEOs from the
outside. Now it's over 50 percent."

In the late 1980s, one *Fortune* 50 company was so concerned about
the inability to grow leadership talent and the shortage of qualified
leaders inside the company that it began to identify and track executives *outside* the company. The CEO and senior vice president of
human resources undertook a confidential, but rigorous, process to
review exceptional executives from other firms—the company even
developed tracking mechanisms on their growth and development.
They went so far as to structure forums—industry task forces, board
presentations, golf outings—to observe targets firsthand.

The shortage will worsen. Aging boomers are beginning to trade
the workforce for the golf course, trading corner offices for porch
rocking chairs, company cars for golf carts. As this boomer bubble
bursts, we will see a 15 percent drop in the number of men and
women of "key leader age"—those in the 35- to 44-year-old range.
Since peaking in the late 1990s, the numbers for this group have de-

creased markedly and will continue falling until approximately 2015 when they will once again begin a slow upward climb. It's a fundamental economic principle that, when supply of a product decreases, its price increases. Companies looking to pay the "market price" for an executive may soon find the quality they want is not in their range.

The second key trend was more difficult to predict. For nearly 50 years, the percentage of women entering the ranks of the American workforce rose steadily. The growing numbers made up for the declining number of men in the workforce. Since 2000, however, an increasing number of women have chosen motherhood or other pursuits that keep them out of the workforce. In fact, female leaders have been departing *Fortune* 500 companies at twice the rate of their male counterparts.[2] So in addition to the overall leader pool's shrinking, women are no longer making up for the number of men leaving the workforce, further exacerbating the leader shortfall.

But that's not all. Boards of directors and shareholders have grown increasingly impatient with leadership teams that do not produce results. In 2001, a record 555 CEO departures were recorded.[3] In 2002, nearly 100 CEOs of the world's largest 2,500 companies were replaced for *performance* reasons, almost four times the number asked to leave in 1995.[4] The challenges of running complex, global enterprises are immense. Modern leaders must carefully manage organizations with large cultural differences, be able to draw out multiple perspectives, and lead diverse teams. Leaders who can do all these things effectively will be a rare, valuable commodity through the "boomer trough."

There is a third pattern—too early to call a trend—and that is the midcareer metamorphosis: would-be leaders exiting the corporate world for lifestyle reasons. This phenomenon is not new ("downshifting" has been discussed and observed by the media over the last decade) but in the post-9/11, post-Enron world, it appears to be accelerating. Fifty-four percent of *Fortune* 1,000 executives surveyed last summer by Burson-Marsteller, the public relations firm, said they did *not* aspire to become CEOs of their companies, compared to 26 percent a year earlier. People no longer see the top as enviable. Career workshops that train people to make the transition from the corporate world to the nonprofit world are overflowing.[5]

As companies recognize the value that superior leaders deliver, they're fighting harder than ever to recruit and retain the best. When Hewitt Associates asked its clients about their plans regarding external leadership hires, more than half indicated they planned to upgrade the quality of leadership talent they bring into their organizations. A McKinsey study on talent found four out of five companies did not have enough talented leaders to pursue their company's business opportunities.[6] So, with the one-two punch of a declining leadership pool and greater competition for those who remain, *how will organizations win the battle for leadership talent?*

Focusing on the Facts

The combination of demographics and economic challenges means that companies no longer have the luxury of taking a trial-and-error approach—or of having no approach at all—to building leadership quality and depth. They want fact-based, tested methods and tools that fit with their organization's culture and support their business goals. They need clear guidance on how to build a diverse, highly qualified leadership team today and how to plant the seeds for great leadership tomorrow. Unfortunately, many companies find that fact-based, clear guidance is in short supply.

Anecdotes and case studies abound when it comes to companies that are known for developing leaders. Every consultant has a model, every conference a seminar, and every leader a story about how a company can build great leaders. But no clear answers exist about what exactly enables an organization to continually produce a stream of great leaders. Why is it that GE had three CEOs in waiting when Jack Welch decided to retire—a situation that would throw many other companies into a crisis? How is it that Procter & Gamble can fill all leadership positions for a growing $43 billion business without a single executive hired from the outside and, at the same time, have 60 P&G alumni in CEO positions elsewhere?

The answers are elusive. Our research discovered that narrowly focused studies on topics like succession planning, executive education, and performance management were widely available, but that no study looked broadly and systematically at the combined factors that enable companies like GE, IBM, or Colgate-Palmolive to be so successful in growing great leaders. And that combination of factors seems to offer the best possible explanation for the consistent stream of great leaders at top firms. After all, it was more than great leadership development programs that produced GE's three CEOs-in-waiting.

When you look at many of the existing studies on leadership, they cite companies that consistently underperform their industry or the marketplace. It makes one wonder: *If a firm can't beat its own peer group, what can it teach others about growing great leaders?*

OUR PROCESS

We set out to tackle the issue in a fundamentally different way. We wanted to understand holistically the organizational characteristics that provide the sustained capability to create leadership quality and depth. In other words, how do great companies combine culture, performance management, coaching, compensation, job assignments, leadership support, and more in a way that enables them to consistently deliver business results and create a strong pipeline of leaders for the future?

We started our research in 2002 by surveying CEOs and human resources (HR) executives at 240 of the world's top 500 multinational companies, posing questions about a broad variety of topics that would influence how leadership strength is built. We conducted hundreds of in-depth interviews with leaders at more than 50 companies. We then sought the input from 25 of the world's leading HR and leadership experts—Dave Ulrich, Jeff Pfeffer, Rosabeth Moss Kanter, Jon Katzenbach, and others—who provided their own thoughts about which organizations develop leaders well. In 2003, we added a global perspective, surveying not only 320 U.S. companies, but almost 300 more in Europe and Asia as well.

To avoid a common pitfall of previous studies, we maintained the basic premise that there had to be a relationship between great leadership and superior financial results. So we passed all data through a financial screen. In our 2003 study, we used the five-year compounded growth rate of earnings before income and taxes (EBIT) as this screen. Companies that failed to perform at or above their industry medians over a five-year period from the study date were eliminated, surprisingly knocking out many well-known firms with reputations for strong leadership programs. Other factors considered included nominations by peer companies and leadership experts in addition to how many leaders from that company were now executives at other *Fortune* 500 companies.

As a final checkpoint, we asked *Chief Executive* magazine (where the initial results of our study were published)[7] to assemble a judges panel to independently evaluate our research. In both 2002 and 2003, they impaneled a group composed of world-renowned authors, business executives, professors, and executive coaches, such as

Jay Conger, Rakesh Khurana, Marshall Goldsmith, Jeff Sonnenfeld, and Steve Drotter. This team studied our findings and made the ultimate selections for the *Top 20 Companies for Leaders.* The lists for 2002 and 2003 are included in Appendix A.

In the second phase of our study, we went back to the Top Companies and interviewed nearly 100 senior executives and high-potentials, including a number of CEOs, to better understand— from their perspective—what makes the difference in companies that build great leaders. These in-depth interviews provided the nuance and subtlety that separated one company's programs from another's and reinforced what we heard in the survey process.

We want to be clear: We know all lists have problems. This book is not about the *list.* This book is about discovery, about understanding what Top Companies do to develop leadership talent. We weren't interested in comparing companies ranked 15 through 20 with those ranked 1 through 5. Rather, we were interested in defining the best. This process was our best attempt at identifying a sample of Top Companies. This book is about understanding what makes them so.

We learned a great deal, and this book is all about sharing what we discovered. Many of our own preconceived notions about leadership were challenged. There are no silver bullets. No formulas or prescriptions. No best practices to steal and embed in your organizations. There are patterns, however, and the patterns are what we were after. The Top Companies share a combination of beliefs and values and results-oriented practices for identifying, nurturing, and rewarding future leaders. These elements form the cornerstones of their programs and set them apart from the vast majority of organizations today. Although specific practices differ from one organization to the next, these common characteristics can be gathered into three broad truths:

- CEOs and boards of directors at Top Companies provide leadership and inspiration.
- Top Companies have a maniacal focus on the best talent.
- Top Companies put into place the right programs, done right.

The remainder of this introductory chapter previews our key findings—the three Truths and more—but before turning to these, a word about best practices.

THE MYTH OF BEST PRACTICES

Managers everywhere are obsessed with the quick fix. Fads and gimmicks abound. The next new thing often promoted by academics or, yes, consultants promises easy solutions to difficult challenges. And this is understandable. Faced with daunting competitive pressures, global complexity, and a nanosecond world, who wouldn't want to steal from the best?

But it doesn't work. Cultures are different. Values and beliefs that leaders hold are different. Strategies, customers, history, and other embedded practices are different. These differences make it difficult, if not impossible, to graft someone else's programs onto your own. It is far better to learn how great companies think—as Jeff Pfeffer, Stanford University Business School Professor says—than to copy what they do.[8]

Best practices, as many people think of them, simply don't exist in the area of leadership. In looking for the easy answer to leadership challenges, all of us have been seduced by books, buzzwords, and even a few consultants into believing that the best way to figure out what action to take is to look to your left and your right, and do whatever they're doing. That's not good advice if you're trying to build leaders. Success in growing leaders is realized by understanding what your strategy demands and what your culture will support and then developing practices and processes specific to your company's needs.

Take it from Larry Hirsch, chairman and CEO of Centex, an $8 billion diversified building and related services firm. Centex is a large purchaser of products from a number of leading companies, and because of that Hirsch occasionally gets the opportunity to visit with the top leadership development people. Many have discussed their best practices with him. Some insist that what they do is universally applicable—all firms can apply these specific practices and be more successful. Hirsch doesn't buy it. According to him, "it's a matter of saying, here is a best practice. Let's take that best practice and really think how it fits our people, and what the needs of our people are." He adds, "We need to 'Centex-ize' it."

So what about all those books, conferences, and consultants saying they've found the universally best way to do "X"? Is there no truth in the concepts they present? Our perspective is that these sources offer many insights into how companies should conduct succession planning or assign leaders to developmental assignments or identify and compensate high-potentials. The challenge in sorting these out is twofold.

First, are they looking at practices consistently used by high-performing companies? We started the Top Companies for Leaders research because we saw too many examples of best practices coming from underperforming companies. One study on succession planning released a few years ago described the practices of eight large companies. Of the seven public companies on that list, all had underperformed the marketplace during the three years prior to that publication and have for the two years since. We can understand that maybe one or two companies have great practices but are showing poor financial results for other reasons. We think it's fair to ask, *if their practices for building leaders are so good, why isn't that translating into better financial results?*

Often "best practice" examples are a matter of convenience. A consultant or academic works with a number of companies over the years and decides to write a laudatory book on them. No tough questions. No rigorous analysis of financial performance. No interviewing line executives to see if any of these great processes ever made a difference to the business. Just a recitation of what these companies do. These stories might sound compelling and worth imitating. But, while drawing inspiration from them is fine, they aren't the place to look for clear direction.

The second challenge is identifying which practices are appropriate for *your* organization, *your* strategy, *your* business challenges. If you're not going to terminate, demote, or aggressively counsel the bottom 10 percent of your leadership population every year, then modeling your succession practices on GE doesn't make a lot of sense. Are you rapidly growing and likely to continue to grow for the next two to three years? Then your strategy for sourcing leaders needs to be much different than that of a more stable business. You have to find what will work for your organization and focus on executing that.

THE THREE FUNDAMENTAL TRUTHS OF BUILDING GREAT LEADERS

Through our Top Companies research, we have identified a number of processes that differentiate the best from the rest. These aren't best practices per se, but they capture what we call a leadership Truth. A Truth can be thought of as an inviolable rule of building leaders—a foundation element of Top Companies. We believe that all three

Truths must be in place for a company to consistently build leadership quality and depth.

In addressing these Truths, we go beyond broad conclusions about what makes companies successful, but stop short of declaring any specific tactic the best. Instead, we provide guidance about the fundamental building blocks necessary to build a great company for leaders and provide examples of how some of our Top Companies have done this. We hope the result is a book that provides you with focused direction about the vital few processes you should build, and guidance on how to build them.

Leadership Truth #1: CEOs and Boards of Directors at Top Companies Provide Leadership and Inspiration

It seems intuitive that CEO involvement would be a critical success factor. After all, the support of senior management has proven to be critical for a wealth of corporate initiatives to succeed. But "top-down support" has become such a catchphrase in recent years, the real impact and meaning have grown fuzzy. "Involvement" takes on an entirely new meaning in the context of growing great leaders.

We heard a clear message from the Top Companies: "Without the CEO's leadership, you will not be successful." It is imperative that chief executives not only support the program, but also actively participate in it, communicate frequently about it, and provide the inspiration, passion, and necessary resources. It must have their stamp, their imprint. For example, CEOs at the Top Companies are intimately involved in their talent-review processes—reviewing top candidates and ensuring their teams conduct thorough, fair reviews of their direct reports, in order to fill key roles with top people. Fred Smith, founder and CEO of FedEx, literally "wrote the book" on leadership at FedEx, and he continues to rewrite and update it every year. When we met with Bob Nardelli, CEO at The Home Depot, he was preparing to visit every division for several days each to conduct business and talent reviews. Leadership development workshops in many companies have a guest appearance by the CEO—at Top Companies, CEOs not only are present much of the time teaching, learning, engaging, and observing, they believe the workshop is *their* forum. They own it.

This is not head-nodding, passive support. It is often a passionate, in-your-gut belief that it's one of the single most important roles for the top executive. And it is *the* way to ensure better results. For CEOs of the Top Companies, that means spending at least a quarter of their time and, in some cases, more than half their time devoted to leadership. They spend the time because they know there is a direct link to results: *Running the business is building leadership capability.*

What's more, the financial consequences are compelling: When a CEO is actively involved in leadership development, the organization averages a 22 percent total return to shareholders (TRS) over a three-year period. Without direct leadership from the top, the numbers drop to an astonishing *negative* 4 percent. Even in down times, these companies consistently outperform the market by 1 to 2 percent. Although that may not sound like much, when you look at market capitalization, it equates to billions of dollars.

Perhaps that's why board members are so dedicated to leadership development at the Top Companies. And you can bet boards will be even more active in the future, coming on the heels of legislative and regulatory reform and shareholder pressure. Highlighting a key difference between the Top Companies and others, fully 74 percent of the boards are involved in the process at these firms, meeting with high-potential leaders, getting to know them both personally and professionally, and learning to understand their career directions and how they think. This enables members to come to the next board meeting and honestly say, "I have a better understanding of the quality and depth of the leadership talent in this organization." Getting the board involved not only gives high-potential people better coaching, but it also keeps pressure on the CEO to continue doing the same.

Leadership Truth #2: Top Companies Have a Maniacal Focus on the Best Talent

It begins with a strong talent pipeline. Many of these companies have built a respected marketplace image, reputations for developing talent, and innovative and selective recruiting processes, ensuring a full and powerful pipeline. Southwest Airlines receives more than 200,000 unsolicited applicants per year; they may hire only 5,000— 2 percent of those who apply.[9] Procter & Gamble brings in hundreds of interns every summer from leading business schools and hires 1,200 new grads globally each year. And they've done this for decades. The Home Depot receives several hundred thousand applications a year. They have the ability to screen applicants online or at computer kiosks in their stores and determine whether to interview the candidates even before they leave the premises. GE sells careers— not jobs—and their reputation as a leadership factory ensures them a strong talent pool from which to select several thousand recent grads annually and hundreds more from competitors, consulting firms, and the military.

These companies are not recruiting and not hiring the best and the brightest out there, but they are hiring the *best for them* and they spend a lot of time and care doing so. Once they've hired their people, they devote the same degree of time and care identifying and developing the best.

Learning that Top Companies focus on developing their high-potential talent should not be, in and of itself, particularly surprising. But they not only spend considerable time identifying and evaluating their high-potential people; they also focus heavily on matching leaders with jobs, providing cross-functional experiences and global or regional assignments that promote strong development. They invest in discovering what matters in preparing people for certain roles. IBM, for instance, not only understands the critical experiences needed for developing candidates for key jobs, but also understands the *sequence* in which these experiences should occur.

On-the-job development is preferred over traditional classroom training because it's rooted in the company's culture (how things are done) and because the learnings are practiced by definition (it's not theory if you're actually doing it). Leaders are matched to new jobs based on development needs identified in the performance-management or succession-planning process. These firms don't just put leaders into jobs, they explain the rationale behind an assignment, describing the specific skill or capability being developed. The company also provides an on-boarding plan that plots out what the high-potential employees need to accomplish at 30, 60, and 180 days and tells them what relationships they need to build during that time period. On-boarding is a popular tactic among Top Companies (74 percent), but used infrequently by others (33 percent).

Sometimes when we explain these developmental moves to others, people get the wrong impression. Make no mistake—these are tough, challenging assignments with difficult goals. These companies intentionally take leaders out of their comfort zone and stretch them to test their capabilities and their capacity to grow. And while support is provided—unlike the Darwinian sink-or-swim models we see in some companies—there is tremendous challenge and pressure to succeed. Being a high-potential in the Top Companies often means you're held to a higher standard.

Top Companies don't pull any punches. Nearly all tell their best talent that they are, in fact, their best talent. While some organizations prefer to keep quiet when it comes to telling high-potentials that they are high-potentials, Top Companies are often up-front with this key population, informing them not only of their status and its benefits, but also of what the designation *doesn't* mean. It doesn't mean they're on the fast track to CEO, for example, or that their status is carved in stone. "Potential" means just that.

Top Companies also recognize the immense value these people bring to the organization. Studies have consistently shown that top performers produce in value at least 100 to 150 percent more than average performers in similar jobs. People who fall into this category should have compensation opportunities significantly above their lesser-performing peers. If they see only 5 percent pay increases, it isn't particularly motivating. In fact, a recent Hewitt study showed the average differentiation for high performers was a relatively insignificant 10 percent. Better compensation isn't an option—no pun intended—it's critical. All of the Top Companies differentiate pay between high-potentials and average performers in the same role. This frequently entails at least 75th percentile pay and perhaps even as high as 90th percentile pay. While that may sound excessive, it's still quite a bargain when you consider the value that these star performers bring to the table.

Leadership Truth #3: Top Companies Put into Place the Right Programs, Done Right

Many firms can build good leadership development programs. However, even the most soundly designed leadership practices can be undermined by inconsistent implementation or lack of integration with other leadership processes. What sets the best firms apart from the rest is not just careful design of the right processes but a relentless dedication to executing these processes flawlessly. From selecting leaders to developing and rewarding them, organizations known for consistently producing great bench strength ensure that every piece of the leadership puzzle fits with the next. In doing so, they create interlocked leadership practices that reduce HR costs, create less cynicism around the process, and make them stronger competitors for leadership.

The best firms also align leadership processes to reinforce the same core behaviors. The behaviors emphasized to a potential leader during recruitment are the same ones reinforced in performance management, professional development, and annual incentives. They understand the vital few behaviors in their company and use every leadership practice they have to reinforce those key behaviors.

Even more importantly, many of these processes are integral to running the business. At companies like GE, IBM, Honeywell, and The Home Depot, talent assessments, development, and succession planning are intertwined with discussions of strategy and operations. It's no tangential exercise.

In our book *Human Resources in the 21st Century,*[10] which we edited with Marshall Goldsmith, several contributors posited that the future value of HR—indeed, the very viability of the function— rests in its ability to integrate its activities more directly into the heart of the business much like supply-chain, technology management, and customer-relationship management have done. Each of these critical processes is a reinvention of a predecessor function that was necessary but of marginal value. Over the last decade, using technology and revamping tired, disconnected systems, these processes have become core to the modern enterprise.

At Top Companies, managing and developing talent is *running the business.* Strategy—where the company is headed, the products and services offered, and markets served—and operations—how decisions are made, and the infrastructure, systems, and processes to support the strategy—are inseparable from the talent needed to do both. In Top Companies, HR builds the systems and processes, but the line *drives* it.

"One of the real differences between Colgate and other companies is that the whole leadership-development program is facilitated by HR but driven by the line," says Colgate-Palmolive's chief operating officer Lois Juliber. "I think that's very important . . . The line owns leadership development, we work with HR to get all the tools, and they put in place the mechanisms. But if the line doesn't own it, it's not going to happen."

These firms have found that the secret to a functionally great design is to design for executives. Including line managers in design sessions, keeping bureaucracy to a minimum, and focusing on getting the results you need dominate these firms' practices.

The result is a company with a reputation as a place where leaders want to work—a leadership brand that will ultimately separate the winners from the losers in the battle for leadership talent. The fact is, for the best talent, it's always a seller's market, and they can pick and choose from the best available opportunities. Those organizations that have cultivated a strong leadership brand will be far better positioned to attract and retain top leadership talent.

BUT THERE'S MORE

The three Truths are important, but they don't quite capture all of it. There's more. There are a number of subtleties, nuances, an intensity and pervasiveness of feeling, small patterns that account for some substantial differences between Top Companies and those below them. In Chapter 2 we describe the importance of the CEO and the board in developing great leaders, but it goes well beyond them—everywhere you turn, the importance of finding and developing talent permeates the organization. It's a way of operating. Leaders and managers willingly give up their best people to grow the organization, to build capability. They regularly take calculated risks—individually and organizationally—to move people out of their comfort zones to test new skills, strengthen others, and build the confidence needed for senior executive roles. This movement of talent across businesses, functions, and geographies creates a powerful web, a network that facilitates learning, a connectivity that fuels speed and communications, and a pride in the larger whole, not just its parts. Individuals develop strong ties and a desire to give back to the organization and to the people who helped them and took the time to coach, support, and provide opportunities for them. In Chapter 5 we attempt to capture these powerful and enduring intangibles.

COMMITMENT 1, SIZE 0

Some readers may feel they simply don't have the resources needed to build strong leaders—they may not have the deep pockets of a *Fortune* 500 company, for example. One of the findings from our research is that company size has little to do with the ability to successfully build leaders. In some ways, being small is an advantage.

Succeeding is more a matter of commitment than resources. The involved CEO and board have little to do with the size of an organization. In fact, in a smaller company, board members may have more time to spend getting to know high-potential leaders. In many of the mid-sized organizations we work with, the CEO is much more involved with high-potential leaders because there are relatively fewer of them. Large or small, at the end of the day, a company's success is a factor of the CEO's and the board's commitment to making this work.

Growing high-potential talent at a small or mid-sized firm may not involve global assignments or formal rotation programs—the organization may not be large enough. The goal is to broaden a leader's perspective on the business and its environment. Leaders can get experience through special assignments, through greater exposure to customers or suppliers, or by ensuring the leaders' jobs are as broad as possible. Larger firms may have a few more opportunities to provide richly challenging assignments, but that leaves plenty of other options for smaller and mid-sized firms to grow their top talent.

One area where smaller firms hold a competitive advantage is in the design and integration of leadership practices. It's likely that the level of complexity and the number of approvals needed to roll out a new process are significantly less in these firms. In addition, there aren't likely to be entrenched bureaucracies in any of the HR functions advancing their parochial views of best practices.

In short, not being a *Fortune* 500 company provides as many advantages in the quest to build great leaders as disadvantages. What allowed the Dells, FedExes, and Microsofts of the world to each establish a beachhead in their industries when just starting out was not sophisticated programs, but the commitment and high standards to have the best possible leaders.

TRANSLATING STRATEGY INTO ACTION

In the chapters that follow, we will delve into these Truths in far greater detail, supported by rich, real-life experiences of organizations known for producing top leaders. You'll go behind the scenes and learn what strategies have proven successful for companies like IBM, Microsoft, GE, Colgate-Palmolive, and Johnson & Johnson, as they've built their capabilities—and their reputations—for growing great leaders. However, this book was not written to provide inspirational reading or serve as another collection of best practices. While case studies provide valuable information that can aid other organizations in their own efforts, the fact remains that there is no such thing as a one-size-fits-all leadership development program.

Chapters 2–5 focus on what we learned from Top Companies.

These chapters are organized around the three Truths and the intangibles that are so powerful in making Top Companies effective at building leadership capability. In Chapter 6, we shift to providing more direction for identifying the leadership capabilities you need and the process for building them. Chapter 7 is a peek into the future—the challenges, opportunities, and solutions that lie ahead. And in Chapter 8, we tie much of the book—its themes, the future, and action—together. The Toolkit in Appendix B provides more tools, checklists, and strategies for turning ideas into action.

Rather than suggesting readers copy what other companies have done, our advice is to read and understand the essence of each leadership Truth, thinking about how you would apply this Truth in your organization. Use the stories and case studies to stimulate your thinking and identify possible challenges. Then use the Toolkit to start creating concrete action plans to lead your company down the road to building and sustaining great leadership talent.

IN SUM

The Gist of It

Growing great leaders has become increasingly important, but clear guidance doesn't exist for organizations with this goal. Our extensive research clearly shows that three leadership Truths separate the companies that consistently grow great leaders from those that don't. These Truths are as follows:

1. CEOs and boards of directors at Top Companies provide leadership and inspiration.

(continued)

2. Top Companies have a maniacal focus on the best talent.
3. Top Companies put in place the right programs, done right.

Facts

- The population of "key-leader-age" individuals will drop 15 percent from 2000 to 2015 in the United States; similar trends will affect most developed countries.

- Companies where CEOs are involved in leadership processes delivered a three-year TRS of 22 percent versus a TRS of –4 percent where they weren't involved.

Quote

"Let's take that best practice and really think how it fits our people and what the needs of our people are."

—*Larry Hirsch, chairman and CEO, Centex*

Consider

- What changes are foreseen in your industry and how does this impact the capabilities you'll need from your leaders?

- Are your practices for growing leaders specific to your company's needs versus "best practices"?

- How committed are you and the top leaders in your organization to creating a sustainable flow of great leaders?

NOTES

1. Jennifer Reginald, "Headhunting 2000," *BusinessWeek,* 17 May 1999, 74.

2. Women in Leadership & Learning, "Why WILL," http://www.leadershipforwomen.com/whywill/index.html (accessed by 2003).

3. Challenger, Gray, and Christmas, "CEO Departures Increase, Survey Says," *East Bay Business Times,* 1 July 2002.

4. "Study Finds Number of Chiefs Forced to Leave Jobs Is Up," *The New York Times,* 12 May 2003, p. C2.

5. Eileen Zimmerman, "To Veer in Midcareer, Away from the Money," *The New York Times,* 18 May 2003, sec. 3, p. 13.

6. Ed Michaels, Helen Handfield-Jones, and Beth Axelrod, *The War for Talent* (Boston: Harvard Business School Press, 2001).

7. "The 20 Best Companies for Leaders," *Chief Executive Magazine,* June 2002, pp. 25–31 and "In Search of Leaders," *Chief Executive Magazine,* October 2003, pp. 24–30.

8. See Jeffrey Pfeffer and Robert I. Sutton, *The Knowledge-Doing Gap: How Smart Companies Turn Knowledge Into Action* (Cambridge: Harvard Business School Press, 1999).

9. Selena Maranjian, *"Southwest Airlines: A Stock for Mom,"* http://www.fool.com/specials/2001/sp010508b.htm (accessed by May 2001).

10. See, e.g., Stan Davis, "Is This the End of HR?" in *Human Resources in the 21st Century,* ed. Marc Effron, Robert Gandossy, and Marshall Goldsmith (Hoboken, NJ: John Wiley & Sons, 2003).

CHAPTER 2

LEADERSHIP TRUTH #1

CEOS AND BOARDS OF DIRECTORS AT TOP COMPANIES PROVIDE LEADERSHIP AND INSPIRATION

Getting the right people in the right jobs is a lot more important than developing a strategy.

—Jack Welch, former chairman and CEO, General Electric

WITHOUT THE passionate and visible commitment of the CEO, developing great leaders is not possible. This is not passive sponsorship. It is a fire in the belly, a near-obsessive belief about how to run the company. "It starts with the CEO," says Senior Vice President Peter Kreindler of Honeywell, who once worked for Larry Bossidy and now for CEO David Cote. "There is a relentless search for the best people and an unwillingness to tolerate poor or mediocre performers in leadership positions. If the CEO surrounds himself or herself with the best people and *demands* that they surround themselves with the best, then that flows down . . . Every weak link means you are not developing people below. But it all starts at the top."

It's not that people don't pay attention to what matters—the fact is, they do. If the CEO won't spend time and doesn't make talent and leadership a priority, neither will anyone else. "What differentiates Colgate," according to Maria Fernanda Meija, a senior executive there, "is that senior management is very keenly focused on people and leadership development. It has to start from the top, and it has to be disseminated throughout the organization."

It's not front-page news that having an engaged CEO and board of directors increases the odds that a process will succeed. It is a key factor in any change initiative. But when it comes to building leadership strength, the CEO's actions and involvement have heightened impact. People pay attention to what gets attention. Leaders throughout the organization look to the CEO for guidance about how to act and about how much time they should actually spend developing leaders. The CEO, as "chief leader," sends a clear signal by his or her actions, and sets the standard that must be met. Lou Gerstner of IBM said it best—"People respect what you inspect."[1]

And when the CEO is involved, the payoffs are significant. It's pretty simple. The CEO's involvement dramatically improves business results. Where CEOs were involved in building leaders, our Top Companies study showed, the three-year TRS was 22 percent—where they weren't, it was negative 4 percent—real proof that investing in leaders delivers financial returns.

This finding was not a surprise to us, although the magnitude of the financial difference was. But the role and the impact of the board did surprise us. Board members' involvement in building leaders sharply differentiates Top Companies. Ninety percent of the Top Companies reported that their board members participated in talent reviews—in other companies, the board participates less than half the time. Another Hewitt study on high-potentials found similar results.[2] In companies performing below the 25th percentile on TRS, only 17 percent had board involvement with high-potential talent, while high-performing companies—those above the 75th percentile on TRS—had board involvement with high-potentials nearly 50 percent of the time.[3]

Throughout our research we heard countless stories of passionate board members who spent time getting to know the up-and-coming leaders on both a personal and a professional level, so they could speak intelligently at board meetings about the quality and depth of talent in their organization. At Procter & Gamble, board members Norm Augustine, Scott Cook, and Meg Whitman regularly teach leadership development programs. Their involvement provides a great road map for companies that truly want to grow great leaders.

So, how do CEOs and boards provide needed leadership and inspiration? We found three key themes in CEOs who excel at developing leaders:

1. They invest the time.
2. They are visible and approachable.
3. They model what they want.

Every company we know says people are its most important asset. This chapter shows how CEOs in the Top Companies make that tangible. We describe what they do, how they spend their time, and how they set the tone and direction for others to follow. Finally, we show how boards at Top Companies are becoming far more active in managing talent and developing leaders. We refer to this phenomenon as the Next Frontier.

INVEST THE TIME

Jack Welch, former chairman of GE, used to say he spent 50 percent of his time on people issues. His successor, Jeff Immelt, spends 15 to 16 full days just during the months of April and May when GE conducts its famed Session C—talent reviews—for each of its 13 businesses. When things were running well, Larry Bossidy, former

AlliedSignal and Honeywell CEO, would spend 20 percent of his time on people—hiring, providing developmental opportunities, and really getting to know them. When he was *rebuilding* an organization, he'd double his time investment. At times, Roger Enrico, former CEO at PepsiCo, would spend 25 to 30 percent of his time just coaching and developing emerging leaders off-site in his largely self-designed leadership development program "Building the Business."

When you compare these leadership icons with how a broader spectrum of executives spend their time, we found a disappointing contrast. *How much time does the average CEO and board member spend on talent?* We asked CEOs that question in the 2002 Top Companies study, and the results were underwhelming. More than half of the CEOs who participated reported that they spend less than 15 percent of their time each month in any activity related to developing leaders (see Figure 2.1). Only one out of every five said they spent as much time as Bossidy. With this low level of visible involvement by the chief leader in the organization, it's no surprise that so few firms feel they are successful at developing them.

For the CEOs of our Top Companies, "involvement" means spending meaningful time on creating the strongest leaders possible. Centex Corporation has more than 16,000 employees located in more than 1,000 offices and construction job sites across the United States and in the United Kingdom. Centex has ranked number 1 or 2 for four consecutive years on *Fortune* magazine's list of "America's Most Admired Companies" in the engineering and construction category. They have consistently had record earnings levels for the last seven years and have beaten analysts' estimates for 32 consecutive quarters.

Twice a year, 36 leaders from Centex's global operations converge on the Four Seasons Hotel in Dallas for a three-day leadership event.

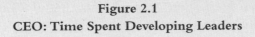

Figure 2.1
CEO: Time Spent Developing Leaders

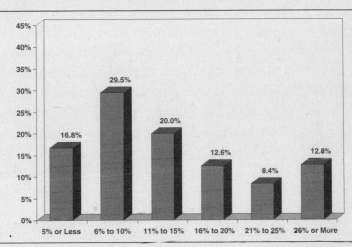

They return a year later for two days to renew their plans for magnifying their personal leadership effectiveness. These events are a signal that the participants matter and, unlike many leadership workshops, these events have staying power. As with most leadership workshops, it's an opportunity for the best talent to understand and to challenge the company's strategies and tactics. But it's also an opportunity to learn what it means to be a Centex leader.

As CEO, Larry Hirsch is an example of a leader who invests the time. During these forums, you'll find Hirsch opening the event with an inspiring speech and closing the session with a rousing finish—but that's standard fare for CEOs at these types of events. What does he do the rest of the time? Hirsch actively speaks and participates throughout the forum. "If leadership is really deemed important, senior management needs to make a commitment . . . What it comes down to is how much time you are willing to spend as CEO," he says. That commitment also means that the head of strategy, the CFO, and the president/COO are all there, further reinforcing the message that leadership at Centex matters.

Hirsch's involvement doesn't end there. After the session, participants are instructed to follow up with their managers to develop an action plan. This plan outlines what they will do to increase their leadership effectiveness over the next year. After finalizing the plan with their supervisors, they then must send a summary of this action plan directly to Hirsch and to Tim Eller, the company's president, for their review.

Hirsch and Eller don't often call their leaders with questions or comments about their plans. They don't need to. The message has already been sent and received.

David Cote, chairman and CEO of Honeywell, shows similar commitment. "I probably spend about a third of my time on people. Whether it's interviewing people . . . meeting with an organization to talk about the future, communicating to large groups, talking with my own staff members about how their organization is doing or the mood of things. It's a big part of what I end up doing and one of the most important."

Cote also plays an active role in the selection of key leaders. "No one goes into a job in Honeywell at a level reporting to my senior staff unless I interview them personally. It's a great quality control measure. Nobody wants to send up compromised candidates and say, 'I think this person can do the job,' unless the person is top-notch. It also gives us a chance to make sure that the top leadership in the company, in a one-on-one discussion, is being imbued with what we think the key messages and values are. It sets a tone for others here—talent matters, and as a leader, you've got to be involved."

He *is* involved. "We just changed our expectations for managers at Honeywell," says Rod Magee, vice president of learning. "It took us three months because the chairman [Cote] was personally committed to refining them. He owns them and he led the charge at the senior management meeting." Cote wants to be clear, crystal clear, about expectations.

Founder and chairman of Federal Express Fred Smith literally wrote—and continues to write—the book on leadership. Smith founded the $21 billion company in 1971 based on a now well-told story that had its roots in a term paper he wrote while an undergraduate student at Yale University. Smith earned a C on the paper due to his professor's belief that although Smith's idea was a good one, it was not executable or practical. Thirty-three years later, the company Smith founded consistently gets A's from Wall Street and the broader business community. The firm always ranks high on *Fortune* magazine's "America's Most Admired Companies" list and their "100 Best Employers" list.

"We have a manager's guide that's the Bible of leadership," according to Larry McMahan, former vice president of HR at Federal Express. "Fred wrote it to begin with, and others added pieces here and there, but it's mostly his writings. He set the stage for our leadership expectations at FedEx. We refresh it every year, and Fred still personally reviews the guide every time we do this and approves it before it's published."

From the very first page of the FedEx "Bible," Smith sets the tone for what he expects: "Federal Express, since its inception, has put its people first both because it is right to do so and because it is good business as well. Our corporate philosophy is succinctly stated: People-Service-Profit, or P-S-P."[4]

Other senior leaders we interviewed at the Top Companies conveyed similar focused dedication. "It's the most important thing," according to Mike Lawrie, senior vice president and group executive for sales and distribution at IBM. "At the end of the day, this is all about the people . . . I spend most of my sleepless nights focused on this—if I have the wrong people in key jobs, I'm in big trouble."

Many IBM leaders echo Lawrie's sentiments, saying they spend at least a third of their time on growing leaders, oftentimes more.

Procter & Gamble's CEO, A. G. Lafley, spends formal and informal time with emerging leaders. He meets with several high-potential leaders—one on one—on a quarterly basis. "A. G. has me shape the agenda," says one emerging leader who participates in these quarterly sessions. "But it is very business focused. We talk about the company, the challenges we face, my career . . . and, throughout, he makes it very clear what he's looking for at the next level of management."

Noel Tichy, former head of GE's Crotonville learning center, states the case for CEO involvement well. "They see themselves as the primary stewards of human capital inside their companies. They define their job as, primarily, leaving a legacy of talent that can carry the company forward."[5] This is a level of commitment we don't regularly see. "Investing the time" can take a variety of forms, but the bottom line is that the CEO must make growing leaders a priority.

Leaders in Top Companies who invest the time provide numerous opportunities to convey and reinforce key messages. It provides a firsthand look at talent, at the strengths and weaknesses of key players—information and knowledge that can be critically important in key strategic moves such as who is chosen for tough, challenging assignments. And it sends a key message that development is important.

"It's got to be part of how you do things everyday," says David Cote. "It's how you think about things, the decisions you make. For every business leader, every person leading an organization, people development has to be a personal issue. You have to feel a personal connection and recognize how important it is to surround yourself with the best people. If you make that connection, I think a lot of it gets easier in terms of getting stuff done."

VISIBLE AND APPROACHABLE

"Personal leadership . . . is the most important element of institutional transformation," according to Lou Gerstner. "Personal leadership is about visibility—with all members of the institution. Great CEOs roll up their sleeves and tackle problems personally. They don't hide behind staff. They never simply preside over the work of others. They are visible every day."[6]

On several visits to Colgate-Palmolive's Park Avenue headquarters in New York, we bumped into CEO Reuben Mark in the lunch line. No executive dining room, no staff member taking his order. He stood in line like everyone else, mixing with employees along the way. Similarly, at Intel, we noticed CEO Andy Grove's "office" only because a staffer identified it from a sea of identical cubicles as we walked by.

Herb Kelleher, former CEO and icon of Southwest Airlines, is renowned for accessibility to his people. One pilot said, "I can call Herb today . . . he has an open-door policy. I can call him almost 24 hours a day. If it's an emergency, he will call back in 15 minutes. He is one of the inspirations of this company. He's the guiding light. He listens to everybody."[7]

We've seen many types of leaders during our years in consulting, ranging from those who take private elevators from their offices to the garage so they can avoid interacting with employees, to those who take every opportunity to listen to and learn from their teams. Top Companies' leaders are out front—visible and approachable—carrying their message, building, developing capability, and coaching and mentoring the next generation of leaders.

Dave Bronczek—president and CEO of FedEx Express, the overnight delivery arm of FedEx, which is responsible for about three-quarters of the company's sales—understands the benefits of being a visible, involved CEO. "FedEx Express has 118,000 employees . . . it's easy to go on FX TV [their internal TV network] and we do that often. It's one of the best ways to reach a large number of employees. It's also easy to send out a letter or memo; however, there's always a chance someone won't have an opportunity to read it. But it's amazing how much better you can communicate with employees when you're in front of them . . . it's the sincerity of the face-to-face that is simply impossible to replicate."

In 2001–2002, FedEx's face-to-face leadership style was instrumental in meeting severe industry-wide challenges. The September 11 terrorist attacks grounded FedEx planes for days. The following month, the fear of shipments containing anthrax-like substances gripped the nation. On November 12, American Airlines flight 587, an Airbus A300-600, crashed in Queens, New York, killing 262 people. The U.S. Federal Aviation Administration wanted to ground the 96 FedEx Airbus A300-600s. In January 2002, jet fuel prices spiked by 50 percent. And to make matters worse, the U.S. economy dragged, causing a drop in overall shipping volume.

You might think that the combination of experiences would destroy financial results and wreak havoc on morale. But something different happened at FedEx. During that time, the company maintained profitability. They also received the highest score ever on their Service Quality Index (SQI), their primary quality measure for tracking the percentage of packages delivered on time to the customer. During that period of time, the company's on-time performance was well over 99 percent, and their employee survey scores—the key measure of the mood of the employees—hit new highs as well.

Faced with serious external threats, FedEx leaders were out in front, galvanizing employees against these challenges. "Instead of hunkering down and cutting everything back in terms of travel, we did the reverse," according to Bronczek. "All of the senior vice presidents and I went out into the field on a weekly basis. We went to Chicago, Los Angeles, San Francisco, New York, and New Jersey, face to face with our employees. In huge workgroup settings with hundreds of managers, we gave them the big picture. Even though we were having a tough time, we stayed the course. Once you're out there in front of large groups of people, carrying the message, it spreads through the whole company very quickly."

MODEL WHAT THEY WANT

Wal-Mart Stores, Inc., the world's largest corporation, is headquartered in Bentonville, Arkansas, but the senior executive team is rarely there. Every week, starting on Monday, they travel all over the world visiting Wal-Mart stores, talking with managers, employees, and customers. They also visit their competitors' stores. On Thursday evening, they return to Bentonville armed with new insights about the market and their people—unfiltered by layers of hierarchy. Back at their spartan corporate offices, they discuss what they've seen and heard and modify their strategies for the coming week. On Saturday, they hold a videoconference with thousands of store managers sharing their observations and providing direction for the coming week. On Monday, they hit the road again.[8]

Jack Welch unabashedly stole this concept from Sam Walton and applied it to GE in what they call Quick Market Intelligence. Bob Nardelli brought the concept from GE to The Home Depot. It's not only a way to stay in touch with customers, competitors, and people, it tangibly and very visibly demonstrates what matters. It's not words and platitudes. It's what the CEO and the executive team *do*—they model the behavior they expect of others.

"I remember being a young brand manager and having an experience with John Pepper, who was our CEO at the time," says Deb

Henretta, president of Global Baby Care, a $5 billion business for P&G. "We were working on a project—the Cheer Free project— and there were some big challenges associated with our recommendation. John had our team present to the executive team. I remember the meeting well—he spoke directly to us, not to the higher-ups, the people between us. All of his questions were directed to our team. I felt I was having a conversation with him. It was an incredibly powerful learning experience for me to watch our CEO go to the people doing the work. It was empowering—you felt that your point of view, your recommendation was clearly heard, and you were given a chance to defend your proposal. At the end, he approved our recommendations and he thanked us for all of our work, but then he did something interesting—he turned and thanked all of the people in the middle for what they had done to help train and coach us . . . It's just one of those moments where you step back and, to this day, I can recite the whole experience because it really had a profound impact. It taught me a lot about empowerment. It taught me a lot about recognizing and rewarding different contributions—the team and the leaders who coached us through the project."

Pepper's legacy lives on today. A. G. Lafley, P&G's current CEO, listens and observes. He frequently visits grocery stores, walks the aisles, asks questions of customers, and spends time with P&G employees. He takes notes on product displays and shelf-space allocation. His soft-spoken manner with employees and customers wins them over one at a time.

But his manner should not belie his resolve and focused simplicity in driving P&G. He has made some radical and symbolic changes. He tore down the offices on the 11th floor of the Cincinnati headquarters, where for more than 50 years, the company's leaders sat in offices of dark-wood, rich panels. It was formal and austere. Today, executives share open offices that are bright, modern, innovative, and equipped with the latest technology. An executive training center will occupy two-thirds of the space. More than a symbol, Lafley expects his team to model the collaborative and open environment he wants throughout the company. He also expects continuous learning and growth—and he expects leaders to teach.

It may be one of those blinding flash-of-the-obvious notations, but the ability of a CEO to demonstrate a strong, personal commitment to the desired leadership behaviors in an organization is a critical success factor. David Cote drives home this simple, but inconsistently followed, maxim. "Leaders who do not walk the talk are very easy to spot," he says. "It's really a matter of how you're acting every day and are your actions consistent with what you're doing," says Cote. "If my team does not see me doing what I say we want, then there's a greater chance they won't do it. And if they don't do it, there's a greater chance their folks won't, either. You have to demonstrate what you want at the top for you to have any chance of having it percolate throughout the organization. I think it does start with me."

A similar sentiment is echoed at Colgate-Palmolive. "It is my ultimate responsibility to 'walk the talk'—set the example," says Colgate's Maria Fernanda Meija. "I cannot ask of my organization, of my people, to do things that I wouldn't do myself. I cannot ask our future leaders to behave in a way that I wouldn't behave myself. So I think setting the example, living our values, living the principles of managing with respect is a key component of what I do." Javier Teruel, executive vice president at Colgate, echoes his colleague: "You can talk a lot about global teamwork, but if the first thing that people see that you do is ignore your colleagues, then you're basically sending a very loud message, which is that you don't really care about teamwork."

At IBM, former CEO Lou Gerstner deserves credit for making leadership development a priority. "Lou Gerstner had a lot to do with reinjecting energy into leadership development. He spent an incredible amount of time on leadership," says John Kelly, senior vice president and group executive for technology. "I'd have a couple of hours' discussion with him on 'who is my replacement,' and for those individuals—and there would be three or four of them, we'd talk for an extensive period of time on each individual, how they are doing, what do they need, do I think they can make it, does he think they can make it, what kind of help do we have to give them to get them over the goal line? Now, Sam Palmisano has taken our focus on leadership to an even higher level."

Kelly, who runs IBM's 40,000-person global technology operation, says this intense focus on leadership is a significant part of current CEO Sam Palmisano's agenda as well. Every two weeks, IBM's top ten executives meet and, according to Kelly, "a tremendous amount of our time is spent on leadership . . . we spend a lot of time on this topic, *a lot of time.*"

This time-investment and focus on top talent flows down at IBM and other Top Companies. Management teams in all of IBM's business units, like their bosses, regularly discuss emerging leaders and opportunities for development in what is known as the "five-minute drill." It doesn't really take five minutes, but it's IBM's way of quickly getting to the point.

BOARD INVOLVEMENT: THE NEXT FRONTIER

If the relatively small amount of time spent by CEOs on building leaders doesn't surprise you, this might. The board of directors in many companies is even less focused on the battle to win the war on leadership talent. According to the most recent survey by Korn/ Ferry International, the global executive search firm, only half of directors say that their boards are effective in succession planning,[9] despite this being listed as one of the largest concerns of boards in a study by the National Association of Corporate Directors.[10]

"Boards ensure the competence and character of the firm's leadership. They can only accomplish this if they, in fact, know the firm's leaders," says Jeffrey Sonnenfeld, associate dean at Yale School of Management and president of Yale's Chief Executive Leadership Institute. "Internal succession planning is too often handled as either age-graded lock-step or a narrow listing of candidates on replacement charts. Even worse is the common reluctance of Boards to trust their own competencies in developing leaders and instead turning reflexively to the search for external messiahs with marquee names."[11]

We refer to board involvement as the "Next Frontier" of growing leaders. Increasingly, board members are taking the time to meet with key leaders on a regular basis to understand their personal goals, their feelings about the company and its leadership, and their decision-making process. Directors are much better informed, and they have first-hand understanding of the business and the challenges it faces and, importantly, the talent it has to meet those challenges.

Randall Tobias, a member of the boards at Kimberly-Clark, Phillips Petroleum, and Knight Ridder, agrees that boards haven't made developing leaders a priority. "Let me give you an example," he says. "DuPont historically has had better safety results than virtually anybody in corporate America. There's one reason for that. Beginning with the CEO, they talk about safety every time they talk about anything. Things that get emphasis tend to be things that are done well, and I don't think the succession process gets that kind of attention in most companies."[12]

It's no coincidence that companies on our 2002 and 2003 Top Companies lists accounted for half of the boards cited in *Business-Week*'s October 2002 "Best Boards List": Colgate-Palmolive,

General Electric, The Home Depot, Intel, Johnson & Johnson, Medtronic, and Pfizer.[13]

General Electric's commitment to building leaders is legendary and they deserve kudos for Session C, Crotonville, and the infrastructure they have built (described in Chapter 4). But what is not as well known about GE is the role of its board. It's their ongoing participation in developing leaders that helps produce a wealth of talent when needed for succession and ensures that leaders at the company don't take their eyes off the ball.

The Management Development Committee of GE's board was very involved with picking Jack Welch's successor, for example. Going back to 1996, they started with 16 names and narrowed it to three. Each candidate had a very specific development plan, and every decision about their careers was made with succession in mind. They were watched like hawks, and Welch and GE's board constantly provided them with "new tests." Directors were given opportunities to form opinions outside the boardroom, through twice-a-year golf outings and dinners with candidates and their spouses. The board went out to GE's business units and spoke to a lot of people. Six years after the succession process began, Jeff Immelt was picked to succeed Jack Welch.

"There are eight board meetings a year and at breakfast before each one, the Management Development Committee meets for an hour and a half," according to Gertrude Michelson, who has 25 years of service as a GE director. "Then, twice a year at the board meetings, we talk about management development. There are plant visits that were usually a half-day or a whole day. There are lots of conversations on the phone. We talk about a new assignment for someone who was in the running. People's eyes glaze over when they find out how much time it takes."[14] General Electric also asks its independent directors to visit its businesses twice a year as a group.[15]

The role of the board at P&G was historically passive. No need for an active board when the consumer giant seemingly ran on auto-pilot. That changed with new CEO A. G. Lafley. "Several years ago our financial performance suffered and we needed to get the board much more active in what we do," Lafley says. "The board now has a critical role in our governance, business strategies, and selection of top leaders at P&G."

Each year, Dick Antoine, global HR officer at P&G, and Lafley review the top 150 people at P&G with its board. "They get exposed to our top talent in a lot of ways," says Lafley. "They not only see them make presentations to the board and in social situations, but also see them in action in their category and country businesses, and even reviewing innovation programs at their technical centers." Scott Cook, for example, CEO of Intuit and a P&G alum, arrives a day early for board meetings so he can spend time with P&G's highest-potential employees. He wants to get to know them, see how they think, how they behave.

Board members also spend time visiting P&G's global operations, understanding its markets, its competitors, and its people—observing the business first-hand, not through PowerPoint. At a recent P&G board meeting in Geneva, members arrived midweek; Lafley divided them into teams and they fanned out across Europe to visit P&G facilities in the United Kingdom, Frankfurt, Warsaw, and Prague. They spent time with the region's leadership, key customers, and the company's best talent. They reconvened in Geneva on Saturday armed with fresh insights on P&G's operations, its customers, and its people.

It's important to Lafley and his leadership team that the board be involved in key decisions at P&G, and to do that, they have to know the company and its key talent. Board members Norman Augustine, Meg Whitman, and Scott Cook routinely teach at P&G's leadership development programs as well.

The Home Depot provides another great example of board-member involvement in getting to know leaders. Each director at The Home Depot is required to visit 20 stores annually. While there, they meet with store managers and employees, listening to concerns, ideas, and suggestions. One director more than fulfills his quota, visiting some two dozen stores a year, usually unannounced. "I'm an agent of revolution," the director said. "This is a crucial board member function, and if you can't do it, you've got to go!" Board members take this so seriously that they actually have resigned when their schedules don't allow them to meet this requirement.[16]

PepsiCo's board members demonstrate similar commitment to building great leadership talent by actively participating in PepsiCo's high-potential development courses. At a recent five-day course, five PepsiCo board members (each a former CEO) shared their knowledge and perspectives on leadership with the group, as they heard first-hand about PepsiCo's business opportunities and challenges. According to Lucien Alziari, PepsiCo's vice president of staffing and executive development, "At sessions like this, board members interact with high-potentials 'up close,' having dinner with them in the evening, talking to them about business, and hearing our people talk in a 'no holds barred' way."

PepsiCo's board also plays an active role in succession planning for key positions. Each January, they review in detail potential successors for these jobs and have what Alziari refers to as "a pretty robust discussion" about the placement of top leadership talent.

Sol Trujillo, a PepsiCo board member and CEO of Orange, a European telecom company, sees board involvement as critical to his effectiveness. "As a board member, I want to constantly improve my understanding of the business, critical issues, our competitors. You can get a lot of that through board room presentations, but you can get even more by interacting with the people who manage the business day-to-day." Trujillo believes that the exceptional level of Board involvement at PepsiCo is the result of current CEO Steve

Reinemund and former CEO Roger Enrico's personal commitment and confidence. "When you're confident in your own leadership capabilities, you're willing to allow others to offer new perspectives and ideas."

At another great company, Wal-Mart Stores, Inc., board involvement is cited as crucial to their successful succession process. "I can tell you why [our succession process] worked. First of all, Don Soderquist [former COO], David Glass [former CEO], and Rob Walton [Chairman] did a very nice job early on getting the executives exposed to the Board of Directors. A lot of people don't talk about that, but one of the things [for] a new CEO is understanding and developing that relationship with the board so we understand what the expectations from the board are."[17]

Boards are starting to realize their importance in the process of growing great leaders. Noted consultants to top executives Ram Charan and Jerry Useem provide great advice on this topic. "Boards shouldn't allow a choose-your-own-successor approach. Starting a minimum of six years in advance, they should demand a list of candidates, plus regular briefings on how those candidates' skills are being tested. As the top contenders emerge, the outside directors have a duty to meet with them alone for open-ended discussions. The larger goal is to create what former Fannie Mae CEO James Johnson has called a "succession culture." A periodic census of the leadership pools at all levels will help spot future stars earlier in their careers."[18] Jeff Sonnenfeld echoes this idea. "Managers with great leadership skills already exist in the firm. It is the board's responsibility to locate this talent and nourish it."

Even the more traditional ways of exposing key leaders to the board can be beneficial. Many of the firms we interviewed allowed high-potentials to give presentations to the board, and others sponsored less-formal ways for the board to get to know leaders, including cocktail receptions and dinners.

CEOs set the tone. Their active involvement, where they choose to focus, and what they do, *not what they say,* reverberate throughout the organization. Managers—even reluctant ones—learn and eventually model what they've experienced. It becomes cultural, a pervasive way of running the enterprise. It represents a core belief, a topic we'll return to in Chapter 5.

Boards will play an increasingly important role here as well. Most executive teams we know have high integrity and a strong ethical and moral center. It is unfortunate that a relatively small number of executives charged with wrongdoing casts a cloud over leaders everywhere. But if corporate malfeasance by a few is a catalyst for greater board involvement in governance, and in ensuring the organization has the right people in key jobs and that there is a strong succession pipeline, this will be a positive, healthy development.

We wish there were many more great stories about highly involved boards, but this is still too recent a movement. As more firms see the benefit of board involvement in building leaders, we're certain more great examples will emerge about these practices.

In the next chapter we'll turn to the target of the CEO's attention—the company's best talent.

IN SUM

The Gist of It
- CEO and board involvement is a clear differentiator of companies with a sustained record of building great leaders and profitable growth.

- Board involvement is the "Next Frontier," with a small but growing number of board members actively involved in reviewing top talent.

(continued)

- Top Company CEOs view developing leaders both as a personal passion and as critical to the future of the business.

Facts

- Nearly half of CEOs spend 10 percent or less of their time developing leaders.

- Companies performing at the 75th percentile in TRS are much more likely to have board members involved in leadership processes.

- Only 31 percent of companies agree that their boards are involved in developing leadership talent.

Quote

"If the CEO surrounds himself or herself with the best people and demands that they surround themselves with the best, that flows down . . ."

—Peter Kreindler, senior vice president, Honeywell

Consider

- How much time does your CEO spend developing leaders? How can you increase this time commitment?

- What must change to increase the visibility and approachability of your CEO?

- How can your board increase the role its members play in developing leaders?

Notes

1. Louis V. Gerstner, *Who Says Elephants Can't Dance? Inside IBM's Historic Turnaround* (New York: Harper Business, 2002), p. 230.

2. Hewitt Associates, "What High-Performing Companies Are Doing to Manage Their High-Potential Leaders," 2003.

3. Hewitt Associates study, "Building High-Potential Leaders," January 2003.

4. Taken from *Manager's Guide USA: The Federal Express Guide to Leadership,* produced by Federal Express Corporation, The Leadership Institute.

5. Noel Tichy, "Companies Don't Develop Leaders. CEOs Do." Harvard Management Update, October 1997.

6. Gerstner, *Who Says Elephants Can't Dance?*

7. Jody Hoffer Gittell, *The Southwest Airlines Way: Using the Power of Relationships to Achieve High Performance* (New York: McGraw-Hill, 2003), p. 13.

8. See Jack Welch (with John A. Byrne), *Jack: Straight from the Gut* (New York: Warner Books, 2001).

9. Korn/Ferry International, 29th Annual Board of Directors Study, October 2002.

10. Report of the National Association of Corporate Directors Blue Ribbon Commission on CEO Succession, 2002.

11. Discussion with Jeff Sonnenfeld, 27 February 2003.

12. Julie Connelley, "Grow Your Own CEO," *Corporate Board Member,* March/April 2002.

13. Louis Lavelle, "The Best and Worst Boards: How the Corporate Scandals Are Sparking a Revolution in Governance," *Business Week,* 7 October 2002.

14. Connelley, "Grow Your Own CEO."

15. Geoffrey Colvin, "Changing of the Guard," *Fortune,* 8 January 2001, p. 84.

16. John A. Byrne, "The Best and the Worst Boards," *Business Week,* 24 January 2000, p. 142.

17. Ann Zimmerman, "Boss Talk: How Wal-Mart Transfers Power," *The Wall Street Journal,* 27 March 2001, p. B1.

18. Ram Charan and Jerry Useem, "The Five Pitfalls of CEO Succession," *Fortune,* 18 November 2002, p. 78.

CHAPTER 3

LEADERSHIP TRUTH #2

TOP COMPANIES HAVE A MANIACAL FOCUS ON THE BEST TALENT

Most companies build their bureaucratic rules to manage the small percentage of wrong people on the bus, which in turn drives away the right people on the bus, which then increases the percentage of wrong people on the bus, which increases the need for more bureaucracy to compensate for the incompetence and lack of discipline, which then further drives the right people away.

—Jim Collins

HE WASN'T prepared for the phone call he received one morning in his Dallas office. As director of customer service at the Technology Company,[1] he certainly wasn't expecting an opportunity to reshape how the company approached its market. The call was from his boss, inviting him to be a part of a project to reexamine the company's mission—an opportunity that would introduce him to colleagues around the world, challenge his thinking, and dramatically affect his career. In his 11 years with the company, he had consistently been pushed to do more than he thought he could and he was used to challenges by now. But this phone call presented an opportunity unlike any he had yet encountered.

Fifteen high-potential employees would form two competing teams, one in Dallas and one in Detroit. Both would be charged with the task of reexamining the company's mission. They would question the company's current course and redefine its future and role. There were no boundaries to this mission/assignment. The world was their classroom; teammates could travel anywhere—from Bangladesh to London—to meet with stakeholders, business people, futurists, government leaders, whatever and wherever they wanted. Under the guidance of a professor from the University of Michigan, these teams would create recommendations and solutions that would shape the future direction of the company. The task was ambiguous—and risky. But, excited and pleased he'd been asked, he accepted.

"Our team traveled all over," says another leader chosen for the project. "We talked to over 100 people. We went to China, Spain, Germany, talked to experts from several renowned think tanks. It was an incredible opportunity to learn about our place in this world. It provided great perspective and reshaped much of what we're doing as a company and now—three years later—I'm still working on initiatives that came out of our work."

This story is just one of many examples we found that support this leadership Truth: *Top Companies maniacally focus on selecting and developing their highest-potential leaders.* They are unabashed about this approach, confident that these leaders and soon-to-be-leaders are the future of their organizations and well worth the investment. And, as the mission project demonstrates, Top Companies willingly take risks with their top talent to stimulate their learning and growth, keep them engaged, and maximize their contributions to the company and, indeed, to its overall mission. The stale orthodoxy of so many companies—that all leaders are equal—is being challenged, replaced by a belief in a strong meritocracy and the relentless pursuit of the highest-quality talent.

Leaders at the Top Companies spoke passionately about their responsibility for and dedication to developing others, willingly offering anecdotes from their own experience. They get it and their companies get it. They couldn't quite understand why leaders elsewhere didn't get it, but they took some pride—almost glee—in knowing that they didn't. It was as if they had discovered some secret source of competitive advantage, available for everyone to see but difficult to replicate.

When we asked these leaders how they would advise their peers in other companies and why and how those peers should implement what they, themselves, have done so well, they were perplexed, uncertain as to where they should begin. You had to experience it, to know it, to feel it, to believe that these things mattered. It wasn't easy for these titans of industry to articulate what they intuitively felt and knew. As we'll discuss in Chapter 5, it was simply a core belief.

In our research, we saw the Top Companies emerge as the rare practitioners of focusing on high-potentials. Despite considerable research suggesting that a focus on the best talent will yield strong results, the number of firms doing this well is small. Barely half of all firms consistently use a formal approach to identify high-potentials, and only three in ten formally develop high-potentials or track their progress.

What makes this point more of a concern is the strong relationship between consistent implementation of effective high-potential practices and the TRS. Additionally, there is strong research showing that high performers significantly outperform average performers and that the differences can be staggering. It can mean hundreds of thousands, even millions, of dollars *per person per year* in value between these levels of performance. The differences only increase as the complexity of the job increases.

Former chairman of P&G John Pepper says, "it all starts with having chosen the right people. I can't overemphasize that. We can give two of our market development teams the same products, initiatives, and resources and, yet, the results can differ by 50 percent. The single biggest factor in that difference—and we know it's true because we've tracked it—is the leader of that unit."[2] Other research bears him out.

Based on decades of research and conclusions drawn from 70 different studies, we know that high performers outperform average performers by nearly 20 percent in jobs of low complexity, but by almost 50 percent in jobs of high complexity.[3] Recently, Bradford Smart discovered that top talent at all levels will deliver two to six times the return of average performers.[4]

Clearly, top performers outperform average performers by a lot. With strong talent a scarce commodity and becoming scarcer still, the lack of investment in high-potential talent in many organizations is difficult to defend.

WHAT REALLY MATTERS

While the percentage of companies focusing on high-potentials is low, the number is growing as awareness of best practice spreads. But companies new to this game often lack the discipline and focus seen in Top Companies. Criteria are hazy, tough decisions are left undecided, and programs and practices grow like Topsy as they attempt to mimic well-publicized practices like GE's Session C. Processes may be in place, but average performers still hold key jobs and block the high flyers. Leaders may have lists of top talent, but they really don't pay attention to them beyond superficial, insincere attempts—dinners or breakfasts organized by the local HR team. Data and information about talent may be more objective, but decisions made are as subjective as ever. It's who executives like, not who is most deserving.

But the focus and attention at Top Companies are different. Although each has the requisite programs and initiatives to support growing top talent, three overlapping themes emerged from our studies. First, Top Companies rigorously screen talent at all levels *and* create a discipline that ensures the right candidates are filling the right jobs. They know what they're looking for in their external hires and use only their best talent to screen potential talent. This is not a task to delegate. They understand that "B" players can't evaluate "A" players.

This rigorous selection process continues once the new talent enters the organization. Emerging leaders are regularly reviewed in performance-management or succession-planning processes and are vetted as true high-potentials by a broad cross-section of leaders, not simply their immediate bosses. The best processes are thorough, objective, and consistent, with the goal of getting these high-potentials the right development and visibility needed to test and stretch their capabilities. And that's where the second theme comes in—Top Companies provide their top talent with a series of challenging, "uncomfortable" assignments. Leaders at Top Companies strongly believe people with great talent need to be taken out of their comfort zone to grow. They need disruption, challenge to build needed skills, and the confidence required at higher levels of management. In a lot of companies, executives who have ten years of experience may, in reality, have only one year of experience ten times over. At Top Companies, they attempt to cram five years into two.

The third theme is a focus on *results*—what people achieve and also how they achieve. Contrary to the (mistaken) notion that some hold, companies focused on talent are not "soft" or paternalistic in the least. The best companies are in fact very requiring. They foster an edge, a competitiveness, a passion around winning. But these companies also strike a balance: results matter, but how the results are achieved matters as much. Leaders of these enterprises recognize that they're building an institution and developing organizational capability over the long haul, and that bottom-line results are not the only important thing in that journey.

These three themes emerge as most important—significant in the eyes of leaders and high-potentials, those who've experienced the practices of Top Companies, and the HR leaders who build and manage them. In this chapter, we will focus more on these things that matter when it comes to developing leaders at Top Companies. Chapter 4 will describe how this gets done—the programs and practices that make it all work.

UNCOMPROMISING SELECTION OF TALENT

In his compelling and well-researched book *Good to Great,* Jim Collins discovered that leaders of great companies first focus on getting the right people "on the bus" and then decide where to take it. If you begin with the question "Who?" rather than "Where?" or "What?" you are easily able to adapt to a changing world. Motivating and engaging talent becomes less challenging.[5]

Leaders of Top Companies are uncompromising in this belief. They are relentless in ensuring the right people get on the bus and the best people are driving. When A. G. Lafley took over as CEO at P&G after several years of poor financial performance, he changed half of the leadership team and realigned their responsibilities. Lou Gerstner did the same at IBM. When Larry Bossidy became CEO at troubled AlliedSignal in 1991, he visited the company's facilities and met with managers and their people. He felt he could tell a lot about a manager by the environment he or she created. He interviewed people in key jobs, their direct reports, and sometimes the next level. It was critical to set the standard for leadership and future hiring— "If you hire a talented person, they will hire a talented person." To help lead the transformation at Allied, he replaced a number of senior executives and personally interviewed candidates for more than 300 positions, the company's future leaders. In a turnaround, it's unlikely that the management team who created the mess will clean it.

All leaders from all walks of life have always known that the secret to success is those behind them, those talented people who aren't in the limelight. Hall of Fame pitcher Lefty Gomez with the New York Yankees in the 1930s was once asked his secret. He replied, "Fast outfielders." The late, great Alfred Sloan of General Motors once said, "Take my assets, leave my people, and in five years, I'll have it all back." More recently, Bill Gates said of Microsoft, "Take our 20 best people away, and I will tell you that Microsoft would become an unimportant company."

"If I were sitting down with a colleague from another company who wanted to build what we have," says Tom Weidenkopf, Honeywell's senior vice president of human resources, "I would say start with getting great people, don't

Challenge Number 1
The Danger of Narrowing the Gene Pool: Developing Leaders for Today, and the Risk of Homogeneity.
The rigors of finding and growing talent can pose several problems. Oftentimes, talent selection and promotion are based on the capabilities needed today, not in the future. By narrowing the gene pool, companies develop strength from the past but do not prepare themselves for future needs. One company we're working with has strong operational capabilities—they are considered one of the best at execution. But as their strategy has shifted to more top-line growth, they do not have the leaders they need to drive the business. Using the Strategic Leadership Matrix (SLM) described in Chapter 6 and other tools described in Appendix B will help avoid this tendency.

The second concern is that,

(continued)

ironically, as companies become more rigorous and systemic in their approach to talent management they may become more homogeneous, not more diverse. Managers and leaders often look for mirror images of themselves. Despite good intentions, the company may inadvertently become less diverse as managers systematically select people more like themselves.

We've worked with a number of Top Companies to ensure this doesn't happen. Building a robust measurement system is key to ensuring that regularly sourced talent is from global talent pools, and that key ratios around gender, race, and ethnicity are monitored. Fostering discussion in talent-review sessions and being explicit about developing diverse talent is another critical step.

start with process. The CEO has to personally be involved in setting the standard."

Leaders at Top Companies have a good sense of who they want. They settle for nothing less. While that may seem obvious, many companies are not clear whom they're after and are unsure where to look. Conversely, Top Companies have the hiring process down to a science. Libby Sartain, the former vice president of people at Southwest Airlines and now senior vice president of human resources and chief people officer at Yahoo!, is often asked how Southwest got its employees to be so nice and service oriented. Her response, "We didn't. We looked for nice, service-oriented people and prepared them for jobs. We hired the person first, not the résumé."

The search for the best people and the intolerance for mediocre performers in leadership positions set the standard and pave the way for Top Companies to build an organization of great leaders. Peter Kreindler, senior vice president at Honeywell, says, "Great leaders have to be great individual performers. You become a great leader only after you become a great individual performer. This eventually flows through the corporation . . . great leaders are chosen and learn from other great leaders . . . 'A' players hire 'A' players, and 'B' players hire 'C' players."

Procter & Gamble, the Cincinnati-based consumer products giant, does not hire any senior executives from the outside. *None.* "With that practice," says Dick Antoine, global human resources officer, "we cannot afford to get [the hiring] wrong. There is no alternative."

Deb Henretta of Procter & Gamble, and one of *Fortune*'s "50 Most Powerful Women in Business" in 2002, describes the interview process she experienced right out of college 18 years ago. "It was the most rigorous process of any . . . requiring multiple steps, multiple meetings, and documented leadership experiences." Asked what the deciding factor was that led her to join P&G, she says, "I was incredibly impressed with the people; they were very dynamic, and I could tell that they were movers and shakers that really made things happen. I was amazed by the effort and resources P&G put into their hiring process . . . they sent 'higher-ups' to campus to conduct interviews with college students." The people she met through the process were strong, engaged in challenging roles— some were already leaders, some were emerging. She *wanted* to join the club.

There is an interesting dynamic between Top Companies and the people they hire. The rigorous screening process and the company's emphasis on the importance of talent breed an intense desire not only to succeed, but also to succeed at *that* company. New hires feel they have passed a difficult test, that they've joined an elite group— they're proud to say they work for IBM, GE, Southwest Airlines, or Johnson & Johnson. And they intend to excel, to demonstrate that they belong, that their hiring wasn't a fluke. This desire to give back, to prove themselves, cannot be overlooked. As one executive told

**Challenge Number 2
Pygmalion Revisited: The
Self-Fulfilling Prophecy**

A classic *Harvard Business Review* article (vol. 66, no. 5: 121–131, 1988) "Pygmalion in Management" by J. Sterling Livingston, pointed out the dangers of focusing too much, too soon, too subjectively on certain people. Early impressions can shape what we observe, and employees carry a "halo" effect so that areas where they excel spill over into managers' perceptions about areas where they do not. "Performance" or "potential" becomes self-fulfilling and reputation, rather than contribution, paves the way.

As human resource systems attempt to identify strong talent earlier and earlier in a career, the self-fulfilling tendency is a real danger. We've seen individuals tagged as high-potential when they haven't yet done anything.

Being aware of this tendency,

(continued)

us, "The company has a responsibility to set the standard, to provide the infrastructure and processes to grow and develop talent, but the people we bring have a responsibility, too. They have to 'wanna.'" We explore this notion of reciprocity a bit further in Chapter 5.

Once this top talent is hired, Top Companies invest the time to select high-potentials who truly are high-potential. They know that if you're going to invest the time and resources to grow leadership talent, you want to make sure you've picked the strongest seedlings.

"Great talent finds me," says Henretta. "As long as you're attentive, they draw attention to themselves. They are repeatedly making a difference and setting themselves apart." According to a recent study by Hewitt Associates, identifying a group of high-potentials is the most common high-potential management practice among the companies we surveyed. Nearly 70 percent of the 125 surveyed companies said they have a formal approach to doing this, but only 55 percent said they implemented it consistently. Our Top Companies' data are consistent with this finding, showing that while 100 percent of the Top Companies formally assess potential for advancement, only 72 percent of the other firms surveyed do.[6]

While that may seem like an encouraging statistic, it's only the beginning of the process. "The good people are easy to spot. You don't have to be a rocket scientist to figure that out," according to Mike Lawrie, senior vice president and group executive for sales and distribution at IBM. "But you've got to have the courage to move those people that you

of course, is the first defense. Careful attention to performance plans and actual contributions—not how they're represented—is another key. Using some form of 360-degree feedback to obtain a balanced perspective and talent-review discussion like Session C will provide a more well-rounded view. Finally, following P&G's lead, described later in this chapter—allowing people more time in jobs and letting them "live with their own mess"—provides more insight into actual performance and potential.

identify fairly early in their careers into the key leadership positions—you must have the courage to put them into important jobs that are important to you. You don't really know them until you do."

FITTING FIVE YEARS' EXPERIENCE INTO TWO: CHALLENGING, UNCOMFORTABLE ASSIGNMENTS

No clearer truth exists about how to develop great leaders than this: Experiences are the best way to bolster great talent, to test a leader's capabilities, and to provide broad exposure to the corporation. At the core, it is about more than just development. Individuals are stretched beyond their comfort zones, they experience periods of

A Focus on McKinsey

One of the best-known factories of leaders is McKinsey & Co., the management consulting firm founded by James O. McKinsey in 1926 and later led by the legendary and spiritual leader Marvin Bower. "The Firm," as its consultants refer to it, advises leaders at most of the *Fortune* 100 as well as many state and federal agencies and foreign governments. The Firm's consultants have risen to prominence in a number of business and government arenas. Lowell Bryan advised the Senate and Banking Committee during the savings and loan crisis. Kenichi Ohmae has become a well-known author on business strategy. McKinsey has produced other business gurus like Tom Peters and Jon Katzenbach. Former CEOs Lou Gerstner of IBM, Harvey Golub of American Express, and Michael H. Jordan of Westinghouse are also alumns of The Firm.

(continued)

trial by fire. It isn't easy. Often, the company actually believes in them more than they believe in themselves.

In his book *High Flyers,* Morgan McCall, Jr. wrote eloquently about the kinds of job assignments that foster unique developmental opportunities: early work experiences, supervisory roles, starting from scratch, fix-it or turnaround situations, changes in scope, special projects and task-force assignments, and a line-to-staff switch.[7] Top Companies work hard at trying to integrate concepts developed by McCall and others.

This movement of talent is not random, but it's not quite formulaic or scientific, either. It's typically thorough and is becoming increasingly so. Our studies of Top Companies and high-potentials uncovered how these companies move their talent to hone needed skills and capabilities. Four themes emerged:

- Challenging people early
- Identifying the right assignments

- Broadening experiences to see how the whole thing works
- Living with your own mess

Through a series of moves, emerging leaders' skills and capabilities are shaped, mistakes are made, obstacles are overcome. Along the way, they gain important exposure and visibility with the "higher-ups" and strengthen their confidence—and their bosses' confidence—to take on tougher challenges.

Challenging People Early

Many leaders describe initial feelings of being in over their heads and feeling ill at ease with their new assignments. The stakes are high and they make mistakes. But they tackle the challenge, and most would agree they learn more from these experiences than from anything else. Most were confident that these experiences were carefully

And while The Firm itself has suffered some setbacks in recent years, few would question that McKinsey produces dozens of leaders who steer the world's largest institutions. The Firm represents an intense microcosm of what we found in other Top Companies—a revved-up focus by its leaders in identifying and selecting talent, training and development, and knowledge management that allow top people to grow and learn. And few organizations can match the number of challenging and diverse assignments consultants experience throughout their careers.

Like other Top Companies, to become a McKinseyite one must pass a number of screens. The Firm sifts through tens of thousands of résumés every year to select a relatively small number of consultants to join them. They target elite business schools where graduates are already focused on a singular

(continued)

mapped out by their leaders and were intended to maximize the benefit to them and the organization. "The greatest learning occurs ambition: to become a leader, somewhere, someday. McKinsey's senior partners are active in the recruiting process to ensure they find the best—to project potential, not just observe what the person is now. The process is intense and requires a number of sessions. Candidates are asked to solve business problems and are evaluated on everything from personal presence to "potential client impact."

Once candidates are invited to join, the newcomers (probably as much as anywhere) are determined to prove their selection was right. Hours are long and grueling. The "McKinsey method" is learned in challenging consulting assignments, regular feedback and coaching of peers and partners, and comprehensive and constant training forums. "You learn what I call ruthless logic," says former McKinsey consultant and Westinghouse CEO Michael H. Jordan. Lou Gerstner elaborates,

(continued)

when you're outside your own comfort zone," says Honeywell CEO David Cote.

Many leaders we spoke to shared stories of being uncomfortable, challenged, particularly early on in their careers. John Kelly, IBM's head of technology, joined Big Blue to be a scientist. Equipped with a Ph.D. in physics, he was attracted by IBM's technical prowess—management and leadership were never in his sights. The problems and challenges he was given early in his career were "huge." "Here I was, a kid just two years out of college, and I was dealing with problems that could have shut down IBM's mainframe business." He worked with some of IBM's best, learned a lot "really fast," and was tested by top executives.

It was uncomfortable, but at the same time invigorating. Within three years he became a manager in a place he never thought he'd be. "I started to realize I could get more accomplished if I had more people working for me . . . I had mentors and managers who constantly coached me, helped me, and gave me the confidence to make tough decisions." The 48-year-old "scientist" is now the leader of the technology group in one of the preeminent technology companies in the world. The group is 40,000 people strong.

At Intel, now CIO Doug Busch felt a similar challenge. "When I was asked to lead IT, the largest organization I had ever run was 100 people at $10 million a year. This was 3,500 people at $600 million a year. I had a fairly high degree of confidence I could do the job, but frankly, I thought people were nuts for giving me a chance to try."

A former investment banker and strategy consultant who is now a senior vice president at one of the Top Companies says, "I had the benefit of a number of intense learning experiences. Individuals who taught me, but at the same time, they expected a lot out of me . . . In these environments—if you're focused and work hard—you'd get five years' experience in two. That's what we want to replicate for our great talent."

These are planned disruptions—purposeful attempts to place people with great talent outside their comfort zones, to provide

"McKinsey had a culture that fostered rigorous debate over the right answer without that debate resulting in personal criticism. It was the supremacy of the idea that was important, whether it came from the youngest associates or the most senior partner. The task was to come up with the right answer."

McKinsey has an up-or-out culture, constantly winnowing its consulting ranks to an exclusive club. Historically, only a small percentage become directors; others are gently asked to leave.

But whether they stay or go, McKinsey consultants and alums form a powerful network—a supportive web of learning and relationships, contacts for ideas for more business and more challenging consulting assignments.

"The McKinsey Mystique."
BusinessWeek, Sept. 30, 1993.

meaningful stretch to build needed skills and capabilities as well as the commensurate accountabilities. A lot of leadership development experts and HR professionals refer to these as "developmental assignments." The term conveys the wrong impression—the people placed in these challenging jobs would undoubtedly choose a more telling name.

Identifying the Right Assignments

While experience is king for leadership development, the Top Companies take more than a sink-or-swim approach to placing leaders in new roles. They carefully plan the assignment, match leaders to jobs, and frequently provide a coach or mentor for support. They take the assignment process very, very seriously.

"IBM forced me out of my natural place—engineering—to work on budgets, profit and loss, and having responsibility for different geographic regions," says Rod Adkins, head of a highly innovative group called Pervasive Computing at IBM. His current team of innovators is charged with figuring out ways to embed technology into nontraditional computing devices like cars, the home, even the clothes we wear. A frequent traveler, one of his favorite projects will allow him to make hotel reservations through his hand-held personal digital assistant (PDA). The hotel will download access codes so when he enters the hotel, he'll never have to stop at the front desk. He will simply walk to his room and through a wireless connection, he'll punch in his access code and enter.

Adkins is leading this cutting-edge group following a series of roles—working on the IBM ThinkPad, other mobile devices, even large mainframes. He's worked as an engineer and as a general manager in both North America and Japan. Adkins believes these moves were carefully orchestrated by managers who wanted to be sure gaps in his development were closed. Based on managerial assessments conducted at IBM's Learning Center in Armonk, New York, gaps were identified. "I won't call them problems," Adkins says, "but they were things that required some tuning and refinement . . . and you then develop a set of actions and plans to deal with those gaps." Some of those actions involved taking a job outside of engineering, and some involved having an experience outside North America or additional education in areas like financial management.

Adkins worked for leaders who made the moves possible. One of them was Nick Donofrio, currently IBM's head of technology and manufacturing. "All of this required a guy like Nick to help in the process," Adkins says. "He clearly saw the gaps and said I needed an opportunity outside of the U.S., so he sent me to Japan. I grew up in our PC business but I needed experience in large systems, so they moved me to the Unix software job. And I'm still developing. Although I'm a senior guy, they said, 'it would be neat if this guy understood our software business.' So now I'm in the Pervasive Computing job." That's how guys like Adkins get to see how the whole thing works.

"Our senior executive committee meets with senior management every two weeks, and we spend half the meetings, two and a half, four, four and a half hours on leadership development," says John Kelly. "The meetings are focused on the jobs that are opening up in the top 300 positions in the company. We all discuss and try to position who are the right people for these jobs . . . And we leave our group badges outside the door in that discussion, because it's about figuring out who the best person is for that job."

"You give people jobs that allow them to more deeply understand what's really driving the industry in which IBM is a participant," says fellow IBM-er Mike Lawrie. "And you don't have 50 of those key jobs. You've got a handful—five or six, maybe ten—it's a small number. So you've got to make sure that your most promising leaders go into those jobs."

Part of the commitment to moving people in and out of roles, and getting them out of their comfort zone, requires leaders to give up their best people. Hoarding corporate talent isn't an option. David Cote of Honeywell says, "Anybody who [hoards talent] is not exhibiting the traits as a leader that we're looking for." Rod Adkins of IBM agrees. "Even when I was a first-line manager, when I saw good talent, I would swallow hard and say to myself, 'Boy, I really need to keep this person.' But at the same time I do have the responsibility to ensure that we are optimizing the talent identified to make sure that we're establishing the future technical or management leaders." Mike Lawrie at IBM further reinforces the point: "For the most promising people in my organization, which is big and worldwide, I don't make the final decision on where they are placed. The people and my peers make that final decision."

Here, risks are imperative for success. "You identify people with potential and you give them challenging experiences and opportunities," says one executive at a consumer products company. "All too often in many other companies, they identify a 'low-risk' candidate for a particular role—one with all their tickets punched, the low-risk successor. When you find the perfect candidate, we'd say it's too late." This risk might involve moving a leader into a developmental assignment that requires moving the incumbent out. This presents a challenge to even the most sophisticated talent-managing organization—"Will we maximize the 'fit' for every key position even if it means displacing the current leader?"

One company's talent review process takes this aggressive stance: "I may have somebody in my organization who is starting to see their developmental curve level off and I need to move them to reignite it. I don't wait for that job somewhere else to open up because it could take three to four years for that. We sit down as a leadership team and say, 'How are we going to free that job up so this advancement candidate can go into this?' In our talent review process, you look at who is available and who's capable and you free up jobs for them."

Broadening Experiences to See How the Whole Thing Works

Modern businesses are extremely complex. Speed, technology, globalization, competition, and demographics make them so. Understanding these institutions, how to navigate, how to lead, how the whole thing works, takes years, and even then, learning and skill building among the best executives never really end.

"There are several things a leader absolutely has to have," says IBM's Mike Lawrie. "One is that they have to get it. What I mean by 'get it' is they have to understand the industry they work in. In the case of IBM, they need to understand technology. They need to understand software. They need to understand services, telecommunications. They need to understand how all this interacts and impacts business. And you must 'get' your own company. You must understand how the whole thing works."

Living with Your Own Mess

With the careers we've described in this book, you might form the mistaken impression that talented people change jobs every six months, and if you're not moving at that pace, your career is stalled. There is no question that Top Companies move their best people into increasingly challenging assignments at regular intervals— broadening scope and complexity. But the pace varies and depends, in part, on the dynamics of the industry.

"We're increasingly coming to believe that it's not the number of assignments you hold in a career," says A. G. Lafley of P&G, "it's the quality of those assignments. It's the challenge of those assignments.

So we like people to be in assignments for three to five years. I know some companies move people faster, but we don't feel we get a good take on whether somebody can live with their results, get through a really tough challenge in that short a time. Anything less and they're auditing the course."

One of P&G's emerging leaders, Michael Kehoe, vice president of the $2 billion oral care business, calls this "living with your own mess." He says he has learned—and the company has, as well—the importance of managers' having the opportunity to deliver on commitments, to have adequate time to overcome obstacles and see things through.

Kehoe provided another important insight: Sometimes there's a need to slow down to speed up. He referred to these as "resting stops"—critical stages of your career, milestones where you're connecting the dots, honing skills, fine-tuning, preparing for the next level. "You may even be doing the work for the next level already, but it's still being shaped. You're going to be leading the battle. We need you to be ready. You may have some of the responsibility for the next level, but not the leadership responsibility for all of it. It's all tuned to becoming the very best you can be at the next level."

FOCUS ON RESULTS

Results matter, but *how* the results are achieved matters just as much at Top Companies. How these companies define results varies, but in the end, they carefully and objectively look for accomplishments and achievements in people. "You may be the greatest guy or gal," says IBM's Mike Lawrie, "you may be the most popular person, people may like you, but boy, if you don't get some results in a relatively short period of time, I'm sorry, but you're not going to be a leader in this corporation . . . you've got to have a real passion for performance."

Over and over, we heard the same message. Leaders in Top Companies are chipping away at subjectivity, separating personal attributes—likeability—from accomplishment and results. But the message is clear: Accomplishments cannot be achieved at any cost. "In any successful organization," says Honeywell's David Cote, "you have to generate results. You *know* the name of the game is about results. But by the same token, you have to get the results in the right way." Javier Teruel of Colgate-Palmolive elaborates: "If you don't treat people with respect, if you don't seek their advice and feedback, if you don't listen carefully, you will basically not deliver the best result. At the end of the day, what we do is as important as how we do it."

Colgate's archrival, P&G, shares this sentiment. "At its core, P&G is a meritocracy," says executive Deb Henretta. Leaders of these high-performing companies place enormous attention on delivering outstanding business results, and that puts pressure on everyone. Fellow P&G colleague Melanie Healey says P&G's search for great talent isn't just about the bottom line. "Number one, do they have the resolve and passion to win? Do they have fire in the belly? Are they initiative takers? Do they take the initiative or do they wait for things to happen? Do they work well with people? Do they multiply themselves through strong relationships with other people on their team?"

This "combination of things" is echoed at IBM. "No doubt some of it is performance driven," says Rod Adkins. "But there are other attributes like the person's ability to get things done, to deal with complex projects, a complex environment, teamwork, your desire to achieve, and your passion around the business. We also look at desire and willingness for self-improvement."

At Honeywell, David Cote focuses on the self-improvement

theme as well. "People need to be learners," he says. "It's one of the things that makes you better."

Like beauty, the "results" orientation is hard to describe. You know it when you see it, but it's hard to capture in words. But there is no doubt that Top Companies hold a broad view about talent. Teamwork, collaboration, passion, and a willingness to learn, to grow, are all part of the calculus. But all of these things cannot replace something that is key, and that's the ability to get things done. At the same time, results at any cost are unacceptable. Leaders here are building institutions, not simply quarterly results.

Careful selection of talent. Regular and continuous movement of the best into challenging roles, honing skills and capabilities. Ensuring that emerging leaders build needed confidence for more difficult and complex roles, while simultaneously fueling their desire to reciprocate for the opportunities given them. Focus on results, real accomplishments. It all sounds so simple, so obvious. But most companies don't do it—or don't do it well. It is fraught with challenging decisions, difficult conversations, holding people accountable, and taking many personal and organizational risks. It is grueling, but these are the things that matter most.

Now the question is *how*. In the next chapter, we turn to the third leadership Truth: execution, the right programs done right.

IN SUM

The Gist of It
- Top Companies spend a disproportionate amount of time and resources on their highest-potential employees.

(continued)

- Challenging assignments are given to the best talent, and successful leaders cite these as critical to their development. In Top Companies, this also means staying with the assignment long enough to see the consequences of your actions—to "live with your own mess."

- The continued investment in a leader must be returned through business results. Development does not occur for development's sake alone.

Facts
- While 55 percent of companies identify their high-potentials, 100 percent of companies in the 75th percentile TRS do this.

- High-potentials are told of their status in 64 percent of companies in the 75th percentile, but in only 40 percent of companies in the 25th percentile of TRS.

- High-potentials are paid more than other leaders of the same level in 62 percent of those companies in the 75th percentile TRS, but only 25 percent of companies in the 25th percentile TRS.

Quote

"You give people jobs that allow them to more deeply understand what's really driving the industry within which IBM is a participant. And you don't have 50 of those jobs. You've got a handful—five or six, maybe ten—it's a small number. So you've got to make sure that your most promising leaders go into those jobs."

—*Mike Lawrie, senior vice president, IBM*

Consider
- Do you know who your top talent is? Do they know?

(continued)

- How aggressive are you in developing your best talent?

- What are key developmental roles? Are they being used that way?

Notes

1. This company's identity has been disguised at the request of the company's leaders.

2. Thomas J. Neff and James M. Citrin, *Lessons from the Top: In Search of the Best Business Leaders* (New York: Penguin Books, 2000), p. 250.

3. John E. Hunter, Frank L. Schmidt, and Michael K. Judiesch, "Individual Differences in Output Variability as a Function of Job Complexity," American Psychological Association, 1990.

4. Bradford Smart, *Topgrading* (Prentice Hall Press, 1999).

5. Jim Collins, *Good to Great: Why Some Companies Make the Leap . . . and Others Don't* (New York: Harper Business, 2001).

6. Hewitt Associates, "Building high-potential leaders," January 2003.

7. Morgan W. McCall, Jr., *High Flyers: Developing the Next Generation of Leaders* (Cambridge: Harvard Business School Press, 1998). See also Morgan W. McCall Jr., Michael M. Lombardo, and Ann M. Morrison, *The Lessons of Experience: How Successful Executives Develop on the Job* (New York: Free Press, 1988), and Morgan W. McCall, Jr. and George P. Hollenback, *The Lessons of International Experience: Developing Global Executives* (Cambridge: Harvard Business School Press, 2002).

CHAPTER 4

LEADERSHIP TRUTH #3

TOP COMPANIES PUT IN PLACE THE RIGHT PROGRAMS, DONE RIGHT

Ideas are a commodity. Execution of them is not.

—*Michael Dell*

IN a nondescript meeting room lined with flip-chart paper in the downtown Marriott in Cincinnati, Ohio, Procter & Gamble CEO A. G. Lafley addresses 28 emerging leaders drawn from P&G's sprawling global operations. The 55-year-old Lafley, a bespectacled, 26-year veteran with P&G, appears almost professorial. He holds his "students" in rapt attention as he discusses the company's strategies and challenges.

More than 500 miles away at Emory University's Executive Center, Rosabeth Moss Kanter, the famed Harvard Business School professor, paces in front of The Home Depot executives. During the three weeks the executives are together in Atlanta, Ram Charan, Tom Peters, CEOs from General Motors and 3M, and other business gurus will don orange aprons and team with The Home Depot executives to provide their perspectives on business challenges and management models for the 21st-century leader.

Procter & Gamble and The Home Depot epitomize the story of Top Companies' programs and practices. These two companies are vastly different, yet enormously similar in what they do and how they do it when it comes to leadership. Except for members of its board of directors, P&G does not have outside speakers at its executive leadership forums; The Home Depot, on the other hand, purposely teams their leaders with some of the biggest names in business. Our research found the "similar-but-different" theme everywhere we turned. Citigroup has a campus-like setting in Armonk, New York, dubbed the "Four Seasons" in reference to the luxury hotel chain—an apt description for the elaborate grounds and facilities. General Electric's Crotonville learning center, a 52-acre campus on the banks of the Hudson River, has been called "the Harvard of corporate America" and is more than a symbol of the importance of leadership at GE. More than 10,000 leaders a year attend programs at Crotonville. Colgate-Palmolive executives, on the other hand, spend three weeks a year traveling the globe in a program sponsored by Dartmouth and Oxford Universities. Colgate's executives mix with leaders from other global companies. They spend one week at Dartmouth's Tuck School of Business, one week at Oxford University, and then a week in cities like Prague or Singapore, common destinations for students in the last several years.

Honeywell has its Management Resource Review, The Home Depot has its Strategic Operating and Resource (SOAR) planning, and GE has the granddaddy of them all: Session C. All somewhat different but with the same intent—to identify, develop, promote, and plan the succession of the organization's top talent. The components are the same, the goals the same. But the programs vary slightly across Top Companies. And the slight variations, the nuances, matter a great deal to them. Leaders of these companies are quick to point out what differentiates what they do when it comes to leadership. They are proud and are always tinkering with what they have. Refinements are constantly added, greater discipline is established, and new learnings provide more rigor as HR professionals and business leaders strengthen their leadership pipelines. Among the many admirable things Top Companies do is continuously search for ways to improve what they do and how they do it—they enjoy a healthy dissatisfaction with even the slightest imperfections. "We can improve a lot more," says Colleen Arnold, who runs a multi-billion-dollar business for IBM. "If we're a great leadership company now, we can be twice as good."

The architects and stewards of these initiatives have a common focus: to identify and develop top talent. For years, leadership development methods were ad hoc and overemphasized classroom training. Subjectivity reigned, and smoke-filled rooms of leaders making uninformed and biased decisions prevailed in many corporations. This informal casualness is no longer appropriate for a complex, global world. Leaders must be systematically developed. "We've learned that it takes a long time to develop leaders and build great companies," says Colgate's Ian Cook, "but bad leaders can destroy a company and the morale of its people in a very short time." Cook and others like him are determined to shift from "leadership by accident" to more thorough, planful approaches to developing talent. "Our objective," says Cook, "is to develop and retain the next two to three generations of leaders."

No small task. Top Companies attack the challenge with the same intensity and deliberateness they do other business problems—whether it be customer service, quality, or penetrating new markets. But finding and developing leaders can be more elusive, less clear, and it is certainly not accomplished overnight.

In this chapter, we share how Top Companies manage the pipeline, the flow of talent—constantly shaping, honing, developing talent. Chapter 3 focused on *what* really matters at Top Companies; Chapter 4 focuses on *how*. To grow leaders, Top Companies use multiple programs and initiatives—far too many to describe here. But we want to share some of the common processes across companies and several of the uncommon approaches as well.

"It all begins with who you let in the front door," says one executive. "If you start with the wrong people, no amount of review, feedback, training, or coaching will make a difference." We begin there, too, and then we share how Top Companies assess their talent, identify strong performers and high-potentials, and move them into challenging roles to shape and strengthen their capabilities as leaders. From there we'll take you inside the more formal learning and development—the executive classroom. Although it's a quick tour, you'll see Top Companies pulling out all the stops to increase the odds that their people will beat the competition.

FROM THE FRONT DOOR TO THE EXECUTIVE SUITE: THE LEADERSHIP PIPELINE

The pipeline for leadership begins with who you let in the door.[1] Procter & Gamble is one of the biggest recruiters of recent business-school grads in the world, hiring more than 1,000 "kids" every year, according to Dick Antoine, global human resources officer. "At senior levels, we don't hire from the outside, so we can't afford to get it wrong at the early stage," he says. The consumer products giant has long believed in promoting from within, and while many Top Companies share this bias, P&G has taken this belief to a level of religious orthodoxy. They simply won't hire from the outside at senior levels. "If this is your strongly held belief about how to run the company— and it is here," says Antoine, "then you *must* invest the time and resources to hire, develop, and promote great people. If you mess this up, there is no back-up."

Over the years, P&G has forged strong relationships with the world's top business schools; they employ more than 450 interns every summer to allow the company and the intern to "kick the tires"; and they rigorously screen every candidate with everything from written tests to multiple, intense interviews. One of the reasons Top Companies are good at developing leaders is that they select for it. "What we're looking for, first and foremost," says Michael Kehoe, who leads P&G's $2 billion oral care business, "is demonstrated leadership, and our promise back is that 'you'll have a chance to lead early in your career.'" Their marketing prowess—P&G has 12 brands with more than $1 billion in sales—has become a breeding ground for leaders, not only at P&G but elsewhere as well. That development begins on day one with the company. New hires are assigned mentors or coaches in addition to their managers, and together they work on a developmental plan for the coming six months. They're placed in challenging jobs immediately.

Honeywell is relentless in its search for talent and believes the ability to identify and select talent is an important leadership competency. They have high standards. "We don't settle if we don't have the right talent," says one Honeywell executive. "We have to love the person if we're going to let them in the door. If we have any doubts, we pass." Their image in the marketplace as a great company for leaders draws smart talent in search of the fast-paced Honeywell culture. Interviewers, which include the company's top talent and general managers who are all well trained in interview techniques, screen for the best of the lot.

The Home Depot hires tens of thousands of people every year and to provide fuel needed for growth, they've created a number of programs to attract and screen talent. The company has more than 1,500 stores in the U.S., Canada, and Mexico, and they plan to open 200 more in 2003. More than 300,000 people tie on the orange apron every day. The people wearing those aprons are a critical part of the "orange experience" that CEO Bob Nardelli is trying to create for its customers. They are the key differentiators. "We have over one billion register transactions per year," says Nardelli, "and if our customers do not have enjoyable experiences here, they'll tell 12 or 13 of their friends. We can't have that." For Nardelli and Dennis Donovan, his executive vice president of HR, it all starts with selecting the right people to hire for The Home Depot. Since they will hire more people than any other company in the world (with the exception of Wal-Mart), they draw on a number of talent pools and processes to get it right.

The Home Depot's Business Leadership Program targets candidates early in their careers. Candidates with undergraduate and graduate degrees are attracted by the company's two-year rotational program. New hires complete four- to six-month rotations—moving through functions, operations, and a Home Depot store. At the end of each rotation, there's a week-long learning conference where participants reflect and share experiences and gain further insight and knowledge from the company's leaders. Throughout the two years, a mentor guides participants. At the end, they are free agents and compete for jobs across the company.

The Store Leadership Program, another two-year rotational program, targets junior military officers, a pool that has been as highly successful at The Home Depot as it was for Nardelli and Donovan while at GE. Tens of thousands of candidates are winnowed down through quantitative and verbal tests, structured interviews, and the analysis of a hypothetical business case. In 2002, for the Store Leadership Program alone, The Home Depot held 33 career forums and received more than 100,000 applications; over half were electronically screened, 4,000 were interviewed, 700 offers were extended, and nearly 600 accepted.

The Home Depot targets experienced retail managers as well—those with four to ten years of experience. Their Fast Track Manager Program has an intense 15-week learning curriculum designed to immerse experienced hires into The Home Depot's culture and operations.

By targeting specific talent pools for key jobs, The Home Depot hopes to attract the large number of people it needs for growth. Programs are geared toward people looking for accelerated development and broad exposure to a premier company.

General Electric hires more than 2,000 university graduates annually from a pool of candidates that gets bigger every year. "We don't back away from that number even in tough times," says GE's Susan Peters, vice president of executive development. "They are our life blood." General Electric attracts potential leaders by selling careers, not jobs. As one GE executive says, "Our product is a future, not an entry-level position." General Electric targets a certain kind of talent. While it has plenty of Ivy Leaguers, it targets non-elite schools or the military and picks candidates who demonstrate competitiveness and hard work, not necessarily high SAT scores.

Whatever the process, Top Companies are careful about who gets on the bus. They are clear about where to find talent that meets their needs whether it be from the military or top business schools. They filter out people who don't fit using technological screening or other tests. A small percentage are interviewed by business leaders. "Our best people know best what we want. 'A' players will only hire 'A' players; 'B' players are threatened by 'A' players and couldn't attract them anyway," says one executive.

Once new talent is hired, Top Companies spend more time and care orienting or "onboarding" them. They know that early impressions, including the recruiting process, form lasting impressions. This marks the beginning at Top Companies. Talent assessments, feedback, 360s, challenging jobs, coaches, mentors, and learning events all lie ahead.

TALENT ASSESSMENTS

Over the last decade, Top Companies have created systemic processes for evaluating and developing talent. These processes had their roots in structured ranking systems of the past, which were used to calibrate performance and determine potential. One executive told us that early systems were used more to "identify the weak" than to build or develop capability. These early models did little to foster the development of talent. Developmental models, if you could call them that, were more Darwinian—hire good people, provide a variety of experiences, and the best will survive and prosper. General Electric, for instance, has had a rigorous and disciplined approach to succession planning for more than 50 years. In the 1960s, one GE business unit even hired a talent scout to work within the group to identify promising managers. The scout concept evolved and in 1967, GE created the Corporate Executive Manpower group reporting directly to the chairman. Group members were responsible for the care and feeding of GE's executive group—compensation, development, tracking, and succession planning.[2] In essence, they were a committee of talent scouts. But in the 1980s Jack Welch, frustrated by the lack of dialogue and candor in the process, had it revamped to focus not only on performance and potential, but also on values, behavior, and developing capability as well.

General Electric's Session C

General Electric's performance and succession-planning process, known as Session C, has been a model for companies throughout the world. Here's a little-known fact outside of GE: Session C was invented by former CEO Ralph Cordiner in the 1950s, not by Jack Welch. But Welch revolutionized it and made it a critical process for running GE. Session C provides a forum for leaders to discuss GE's talent and the opportunities to strengthen it, but as importantly, it provides a place for candor and debate, for calibration of standards and business priorities, and the reinforcement of cultural norms and values. In the 1980s, Welch became concerned about the intense focus on results at GE that encouraged managers to run roughshod over employees. In Welch's new world at GE, making the numbers became the ticket to admission; adhering to the company's values, on the other hand, drove career advancement.

The process begins every January when hundreds of thousands of GE employees complete an online self-assessment list their

Challenge Number 3
To Rank or Not

There are few topics around managing talent that engender fiercer debate than forced ranking. Many companies rank their employees either explicitly or implicitly, behind closed doors. GE is the most notable and visible company that ranks employees, but surveys show about 20 percent of companies rank, and the percentage appears to be growing.

Proponents argue there is no better way to truly calibrate performance across business units and functions. Ranking reduces the rating inflation that characterizes so many performance management systems and does a better job of differentiating the best—and the worst—from the rest.

Those who oppose these processes say they are nothing more than systems to identify the weak, not vehicles to pro-

(continued)

accomplishments, adherence to GE's values, their developmental goals, and career aspirations. At the same time, they update their internal resumes—jobs they've held and educational experiences—

mote high performance. The yearly spasm substitutes for a process that should be ongoing, regular, and more consistent. Ranking disrupts teamwork and pits employees against one another. It penalizes high-performing groups as managers are forced to identify the worst of the best. Critics further argue that it's stressful for managers and employees and causes managers to underinvest in the development and coaching of average or mediocre perform-ers—which is exactly what the employees need. Furthermore, ranking may lead to legal expo-sure, as Ford Motor Company discovered when it had to aban-don its forced ranking process when it was hounded by lawyers from the American Association of Retired Persons who claimed the process discriminated against older workers.

As with many things in talent management, there is no right answer. Ranking can and does

(continued)

used for GE's global internal-posting system. Supervisors and managers complete a similar evaluation on each employee and then meet for an open dis-cussion.

These individual evaluations flow upward, in a reverse cas-cade, through every department, function, geography, and busi-ness unit. Managers and leaders of departments meet and discuss unit-by-unit the talent they have and the talent they need. In May of each year, CEO Jeff Immelt visits each of GE's 13 business units for full-day Session C meetings, starting in the early morning and ending late into the night. The dialogue is rich and open. Talent discussions on GE's top 500 positions are inter-twined with business challenges, needs, and key initiatives like Six Sigma, digitalization, or the commercial or marketing side of GE. These strategic priorities are inseparable from the discussion of talent.

But the focus is clearly on the *development* of leaders to meet the business challenges ahead. Immelt probes and questions as every top executive is discussed. "Do people like working for her?" he will ask. "Who has she brought along? What does he want to do next?" If the executive is ready for a move, Bill Conaty, GE's vice president of HR, and Susan Peters facilitate cross-business assignments.

In July, Immelt and Conaty conduct a videoconference with heads of the business units and their HR leaders to gauge progress on the May decisions. The public review and visibility are no accident. Follow-up and accountability are part of the DNA of high-performing companies, and GE has been a charter member of that club for decades. Progress is checked again in the fall during operating review sessions.

The process is an integral part of running GE's $130 billion business. The discussion of talent throughout GE follows strategic reviews of each business and the key strategic initiatives shared with top management at GE's annual meeting in January, held in Boca Raton, Florida, for the top 600 executives. Following Boca, Peters and Conaty develop the agenda for Session C discussions to

work for some companies. Where there is rigor and regular and consistent performance discussions and employees know the rules of the road, it can be quite effective. Sometimes it's a matter of timing, too. We will advise clients needing forced discipline around performance and where there's some time urgency, that ranking may be an appropriate intervention until business conditions change and/or performance discussions become more normative. In these situations, managers need lots of training and support, facilitated talent-review discussions by either consultants or HR professionals, and strong communications with all employees.

But there are many situations where ranking simply is not appropriate. It may be counter cultural, inconsistent with established values and beliefs; or the disruption may not be worth the pain. Even here, however,

(continued)

the question remains—how to differentiate different levels of contribution? Many companies take the approach that performance should be evaluated against established goals and job responsibilities. This allows managers to keep motivation high by assessing people against agreed-upon goals and objectives. These companies may then stipulate some differentiation on *pay* but not the performance rating.

be held in the business units in the coming months. "Think about half the session focusing on the review of talent, the other half on the talent and organizational capability needed for the key business issues flowing out of Boca," says Peters. Strategy, talent, and operations are all intertwined, connected.

General Electric's formula for winning the war for talent is not that complicated, but few have achieved and sustained what GE has for so long. Their building blocks are simple: Hire outstanding talent, create an intense performance culture, and rigorously assess performance and promotability. Just words to many. But at GE, they back it up. They continuously evaluate performance, both formally and informally, and ensure differentiation in pay and opportunities between the best and the least effective. They sell careers and they have the infrastructure—and the discipline—to do what they say they'll do.

Strategic Operating and Resource Planning at The Home Depot

The Home Depot's CEO Bob Nardelli and executive vice president of HR Dennis Donovan are both GE alums, so it's not surprising that they brought what they learned from the company that "brings good things to life" to the $60 billion home improvement business. "I was tremendously advantaged by the experience at GE," says Nardelli.

"The processes we developed and applied there were a wonderful learning laboratory."

Strategic Operating and Resource Planning is not just a convenient acronym—SOAR—but rather the key process to running The Home Depot. Having a vision is not enough for Nardelli. Weaving together strategy, operations, and resources—specifically talent—is the solution.

Every spring, Nardelli and Donovan visit each Home Depot division for intensive business and talent reviews. The day begins at 7:00 A.M. with an overview of the regional business, the communities served, and a detailed discussion of the division's top management. The remainder of the morning is spent discussing the leadership pipeline, staffing, retention, and store leadership. Nardelli uses these opportunities to learn about the business, to listen, but also to drive his message home. "One of the most important things for us as leaders is to select and surround ourselves with people who can carry out our vision," he says. "If we don't lead, they can't follow. If we don't coach, they can't play . . . and if they don't play, we can't win." He's intensely disciplined and engaged in discussions and evaluations of The Home Depot's people. "He takes this very seriously," says Carol Tome, The Home Depot's intense CFO. "He will send you back comments on evaluations, he will challenge you about raising the bar or more aggressively moving people into stretch roles."

Nardelli, Donovan, and other leaders at The Home Depot lunch with high-potentials and emerging talent. Nardelli's noncharismatic but nonetheless engaging style is motivating to those who attend. "I'll follow him off a cliff," says one.

The afternoon includes more discussions on learning initiatives, diversity, and developmental assignments for strong performers with potential. The day ends with a town hall meeting for several hundred employees that Donovan describes as a combination of a "love in" and a "food fight," as love for the company (and increasingly, for Nardelli) mixes with open dialogue and no-holds-barred candor. Donovan calls the day a "hoot"—the CEO gets to put his finger on the pulse of the company, learn about the business and community, convey and reinforce key messages, and have some fun—all in one day. At the end of the process, Nardelli and Donovan will have discussed thousands of Home Depot employees and will have carried their message to tens of thousands more.

Colgate-Palmolive's Human Resources Committee

Once a month, Bill Shanahan, Colgate's president, chairs a small committee of the company's top executives. Lois Juliber, chief operating officer; Javier Teruel, executive vice president; Ian Cook, executive vice president; Bob Joy, senior vice president of HR; and Shanahan's head of global people development and staffing, Coleen Smith, are all present. "We don't try to get too fancy," says Joy, whose words are still tinged with a Tennessee accent. For half a day each month this group—known as Colgate-Palmolive's Human Resources Committee (CPHR)—gets updates on global moves, makes decisions on candidates for key positions worldwide, and talks about people who need moves. They acknowledge that they wander a bit, but important work gets done. They have final say on the company's high-potential lists and on which people will move into challenging job assignments.

"It's done at the top of the house," says Juliber, "and that sends a signal that it's important." The CPHR is responsible for global oversight, but much like GE and The Home Depot, the process begins with Individual Development Plans, or one-on-one discussions with managers, and bubbles up into management review sessions for every division, function, and geography in the company. And these sessions are conducted not once, but twice a year.

Like many Top Companies, Colgate has rich data and information on each person discussed—job history, education, performance reviews, development needs, and preferences. And, like many others, Colgate's data are all automated in databases that allow global searches and permit greater analyses of talent needs.

Several companies supplement these talent reviews with additional data—results from assessment centers conducted by the Center for Creative Leadership in Greensboro, North Carolina, by DDI in Pittsburgh, or by a host of other leadership evaluators. One Top Company goes a step further. Their talent review begins in June, but they carefully point out they do not do succession planning, which they refer to as "filling deadmen's boots." "We believe it's important to think about moves and develop capability well before a vacancy is created," says the senior vice president of HR.

All Top Companies have similar models. Many of the executives we spoke with were old enough to remember predecessor processes such as the more-bureaucratic replacement planning. "We'd spend countless hours and huge amounts of staff time developing depth charts for every position in the company," one seasoned veteran told us. "It was a waste of time." Today the world moves too fast, roles change, and targeting individuals for specific jobs makes little sense. Top Companies think more of talent or acceleration *pools* to draw from when jobs open up.

To supplement its twice-yearly, several-day-long talent review sessions, one company uses what they call "Executive Check-Ins." The company's top leaders identify promotable people and then two other direct reports of the top manager are charged with spending four to six hours with the candidates. In these sessions they review

Challenge Number 4
High-Potentials:
Should You Tell?

There is one question that senior leaders everywhere toil over year after year: Should you inform high-potentials of their status? Believe it or not, more companies tell high-potentials than not, but it is often implicit— with a wink and a nod—rather than a clear and explicit message. When asked if he would tell high-potentials of their status, Larry Bossidy, former CEO of AlliedSignal and Honeywell, replied, "No, not explicitly. Certainly it is fine to tell people they are doing a good job and we think they have a lot of potential. I wouldn't tell them we think you are one of the top ten people in the business. I think that's unnecessary and perhaps ineffective."

Leaders offer several reasons for their discomfort. First, in many companies, the criteria around high-potentials are very subjective, and it's difficult to differentiate high performance from potential. (Appendix B contains an extensive discussion about the difference between

(continued)

accomplishments, work product, and development goals. They write a short report, return, and provide feedback to the individual and, later, to his or her manager. "It is not viewed as threatening," but rather as helpful, says the head of HR. "It is seen as developmental and has the byproduct of having other senior leaders getting exposure to talent they wouldn't otherwise see."

These Executive Check-Ins are similar to the Accomplishment Analysis initiated by the Executive Manpower Group at GE. In a process now called Executive Assessments, two-person HR teams provide a 10- to 15-page report containing a detailed appraisal of an individual's strengths, weaknesses, and suggested developmental moves. They spend four to five hours with each candidate and conduct a 360-degree "reference check," talking to as many as 30 people. Following a review with the executive and his or her manager, the report goes to both Jeff Immelt and Bill Conaty. IBM does

Executive Interviews, or "EIs." They provide opportunities for executives to get to know talent outside their own group. "I take a very active role in this," says IBM's Colleen Arnold. "I spend a lot of time on talent, maybe three to four discussions per week. So when my managers tell me who emerging leaders are, I know these people first-hand."

Both processes are focused on development and provide a broader peek at talent outside the chain of command.

Whatever the process, Top Companies are committed to understanding and developing their talent. The time and resources devoted to these efforts are sometimes daunting, but Bob Nardelli at The Home Depot, Reuben Mark at Colgate, Fred Smith at FedEx, David Cote at Honeywell, Sam Palmisano at IBM, A. G. Lafley at P&G, and Jeff Immelt at GE can't all be wrong. "These are *investments* and that's the way we see it," says one, "and they are investments that you cannot *not* make." Carol Tome, CFO at The Home De-

performance and potential.) And organizations need both. Second, leaders are concerned about what to do if someone is no longer high-potential. Do they come off the list?

In general, we think it's best to let high-potentials know their status when you're confident you've accurately identified them and there are real consequences to this status. The concerns raised are valid but create an opportunity for clarity and more rigor around distinguishing high-potentials from high performers. It also creates an opportunity to better prepare managers for discussions around potential: what it means, how it's demonstrated, and the circumstances in which someone may lose the designation.

Lawrence A. Bossidy and Marcia J. Avedon. 2002. Getting an executive view: An interview with a chief executive officer. In The 21st century executive: Innovation practices for building leadership at the top, *ed. Rob Silzer, 2001. San Francisco: Jossey-Bass.*

pot, says, "It's worth every penny and every minute of time. You can *see* the return. I *know* what it costs. I write the checks."

IDENTIFYING EMERGING LEADERS AND HIGH-POTENTIALS

The talent assessment—by whatever name—is a critical process for Top Companies to identify their best performers and those with the highest potential.

As we noted in Chapter 3, another Hewitt study on high-potential leaders found that most organizations focus very little attention on this critically important talent pool. Planned development of high-potentials occurs at only three in ten companies, and inconsistency reigns in everything from identifying high-potentials, to informing them, to having formal processes to develop them.

Top Companies are clearer when it comes to high-potentials. And, while many leaders we spoke with acknowledged definitions are still too fuzzy and subjective, they are working hard to tighten them. First and foremost, to be considered a high-potential, you must be a high performer. "You can't get on these lists," says GE's Susan Peters, "unless you demonstrate results—you get stuff done." After that, leaders look at a number of factors: the ability and willingness to learn and grow, the tendency to expand the scope of past jobs to create more value, and a relatively steep slope demonstrated in mastering previous roles and assignments. "At GE, we want to know whether the person can lead teams, do people follow them, can they influence across business groups?" says Peters. As a final test in many Top Companies, the question is asked, *Can we envision the candidate in a role at the next level within two years?*

Some companies use an application to initiate the process of identifying high-potentials. At one retail pharmacy company, managers—

the candidates themselves—who meet certain requirements apply for the high-potential program. Applications are reviewed by the next two levels of management. Managers are selected for one-year increments and must reapply each year.

But most Top Companies use the talent-review process to select key talent. Candidates are typically plotted into a nine-block grid along two dimensions—performance and potential. Development plans then are tailored for each individual no matter where he or she is placed on the nine block, as it's called. Individuals designated as high-potential often get special attention for fast-track jobs and development and learning opportunities, as well as aggressive pay treatment and even stock options or grants. We provide further discussions and examples of the nine block in Appendix B.

IBM's Senior Leadership Group and the NextGens

In February 1995, IBM's then-CEO Lou Gerstner formed the Senior Leadership Group (SLG)—the top 300 executives—to focus attention on leadership and change. Gerstner saw this group as change agents for IBM's transformation and, for that reason, he felt membership needed to be earned, not granted automatically. It would not be based on role, rank, or tenure. Every year his executive team performed triage on the group—some people would retire, some people would be asked off, and new people added. There's a lot of turnover in the SLG. Of the original 300 in 1995, only 71 remained at the meeting in March 2002.[3]

Every year, the CEO hosts a meeting of the SLG. And for several days, they review the company's strategies, competitive situation, and key initiatives. But a significant chunk of time is devoted to leadership. IBM's talent-review process—much like the ones described in the previous pages—is a critical process for identifying the SLG and IBM's highest-potential employees. But IBM is a big, complex enterprise with more than 300,000 employees. "Digging down in the organization and finding great talent is a difficult thing to do," says Donna Riley, vice president of global executive resources and development at IBM. "So in 2002, we asked the SLG to reach down in their organization and find a young person with less than ten years of work experience who could someday sit in their chairs. Nothing more than that," says Riley. "No fancy assessment or identification process and [the SLG] responded with enormous enthusiasm and are now sponsors of this group we call our 'NextGens.'"

NextGens are assigned coaches to assist in their accelerated development. They are given the opportunity to attend IBM's Advanced Leaders Series, composed of two classes: the Global Development Center and Global Business Management. They receive 360-degree feedback and are evaluated in a number of simulations by members of the SLG.

Like many Top Companies, IBM uses several channels to identify and develop their best talent. Another channel is their Executive Assistant Program.

IBM's Executive Assistant Program

NextGens are the key talent pool for another IBM initiative, its Executive Assistant Program. Executive Assistants serve as the "right-hand staff" for IBM's top global executives. The company's Worldwide Management Council—the top 52 executives, plus eight other general managers of IBM's largest markets—hand-picks assistants and provides them with broad exposure to the business, its leaders, and the company's most challenging business problems.

These jobs are relatively short, 9 to 12 months, but provide invaluable exposure for emerging talent. And that exposure goes both ways. Leaders observe their pipeline first-hand and provide another opportunity to calibrate IBM's global workforce. In the last several years, Randy MacDonald, IBM's executive vice president of HR, has drawn his Executive Assistants from North Carolina, the United Kingdom, and Japan. "It's important that we tap our strongest people from all over the world and work directly with them and give them the right exposure," says MacDonald. "It also forges a strong network across IBM and that's a lot of who we are as a company." Assistants are provided a coach and a program manager who guide developmental goals and key learnings. It has been an important step for a number of IBM's top executives—current CEO Sam Palmisano was an assistant to former CEO John Akers, and marketing head Abby Kohnstamm assisted Lou Gerstner. Colleen Arnold was an assistant to sales chief Mike Lawrie. Rod Adkins, head of Pervasive Computing, was also an executive assistant at one point in his career.

Challenge Assignments

Joanna Murphy[4] was born in the Middle East, educated in Switzerland, and, following her university studies in London, she joined Captiva Cosmetics[5] as a marketing trainee, a "junior nitwit," as she calls it. Early in her 22-year career with Captiva, she progressed through the ranks in marketing—product manager, senior product manager, and so on—and after six years in Ireland, she was asked to come to corporate headquarters in Chicago to be a part of a team to help shape the company's global evolving strategy.

After two and a half years in Chicago, Murphy became the marketing director for the Philippines, where, in three years, she experienced one revolution and five coup attempts. She then moved to Latin America. Prior to taking on her first general manager job in the Dominican Republic, she labored hard to pick up a second language—she took Spanish lessons from a Cuban teacher—only to discover Dominican Spanish is completely different from Cuban

Spanish. A hard lesson of our global economy. After 18 months in Latin America, Murphy became president of a small acquisition in Dallas, Texas and was charged with integrating it with two other acquisitions—one in California, the other in Atlanta—and creating one of Captiva's biggest businesses. She ultimately had to close down the Dallas facility as they consolidated operations. She found this painful, and she personally met with every person they let go to offer them jobs in other Captiva locations. Most didn't take the offer, but she felt compelled to meet with them. From there it was off to Milan as general manager for Italy. After 18 months, she received a call from the CEO asking her to once again come to Chicago to help turn around a business that was losing ground to competitors.

Murphy ultimately landed the company's top marketing job and later became head of the Americas and Europe. In her nearly 25 years with the company, she has had leadership roles in every region of the world, has managed rapid growth, turnarounds, mergers, start-ups, shutdowns, and staff jobs. One of her children was born in Chicago, the other in Manila. During the revolution in the Philippines, she had to balance concerns about the safety of her family with her leadership responsibilities. Many companies whisked their expats to Hong Kong. Murphy and her family stayed. No training program, book, or mentor could possibly have created the same intense understanding and feeling of geopolitical risks experienced by Murphy.

While in the Dominican Republic, a young Stanford-graduated, female executive working for Murphy was killed when she resisted a burglary in her apartment. Murphy experienced, at a very emotional time, the powerful effect she could have as a leader. Murphy helped the family through their trauma and in the course of many discussions with the young woman's parents, they provided details of their daughter's exchanges with her—the dinners Murphy and her family had invited her to. "They could relay conversations, they knew the names of our kids," she recalled. "The personal learning for me, as a leader, is that you have to give of yourself and become accessible to people. People follow a variety of things," she went on, "but at the end, they feel a connection with a value system and I think we as leaders must emulate that."

Murphy also experienced Captiva's value system. Following the young woman's death, Captiva's CEO immediately arranged for the company jet to fly her parents to the Dominican Republic. The CEO and Murphy both attended the funeral in Tucson, Arizona.

"I really felt part—and proud—of an organization that was expressing its values in a time of crisis," Murphy said. Murphy's experiences, both positive and negative, are part accident, part luck, and part planned. As we spoke with leaders across a number of companies, they relived similar careers. Many believed someone was moving the chess pieces, orchestrating the movements to hone the capabilities and experiences that produce great leaders. But they also acknowledge that some of it was fortuitous, accidental, or just plain luck.

Of all the things that contribute to producing great leaders, job experiences—diverse job experiences, to be specific—rank number one. And, as grand masters of today's chess game, the leaders of Top Companies have set out to more systematically create the right moves for more of the right people. "Our world is too big, too complex, too fast-moving to leave it in the hands of informal, 'good old boy' networks. We'd miss too many people, too many opportunities," one person told us.

Helping to Plan Assignments at IBM

"Eighty percent of development happens on the job," says IBM's Donna Riley. "Learning has to be grounded in the real world. That's why we focus on what job assignments people go into and provide them with strong coaching. Leaders teach other leaders."

Riley and her team have developed sophisticated tools and models to determine the right moves, and when to make them. Like many Top Companies, IBM has a set of leadership competencies, developed in 1996 and revalidated in 1999, that help guide the right moves (see Figure 4.1). Gerstner supported these efforts. He saw this as a vehicle to accelerate his transformation of IBM—to promote and reward executives who embraced the new IBM. Like many companies, these competencies were developed by understanding the skills, capabilities, and traits of IBM's best people. The competencies cluster around four areas:

- *Focus to Win.* Understanding the business environment moment to moment and setting strategies for breakthrough results.

Figure 4.1
IBM Leadership Competencies

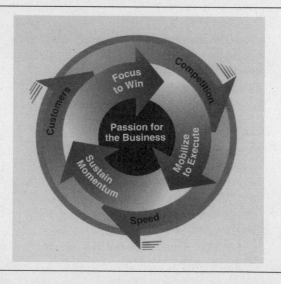

- *Mobilize to Execute.* Implementing with speed, flexibility, and teamwork.
- *Sustain Momentum.* Obtaining lasting results that continue to grow.
- *Passion for the Business.* Being excited about what IBM technology and services can do for the world. This passion for the business and winning in the marketplace is at the core of IBM's Leadership Model.

Similar to a lot of other Top Companies, each of the areas is broken down into competencies—in total, a set of 11.

Focus to Win
- Customer Insight
- Breakthrough Thinking
- Drive to Achieve (entrepreneur-like hunger)

Mobilize to Execute
- Team Leadership
- Straight Talk
- Teamwork
- Decisiveness

Sustain Momentum
- Building Organizational Capability
- Coaching
- Personal Dedication (IBM first)

The Core
- Passion for the Business

But Gerstner was not satisfied. While changes were taking place at IBM, the cultural side was stagnant. He felt these principles and competencies needed to be simpler and embedded into what people did every day. He broke these down further to "Win, Execute, Team." This mantra—short, tight, clear—spread throughout IBM and became a critical part of many IBM programs and initiatives.

Not too surprising so far. We've all seen these themes, phrases, the focused simplicity of a broader set of competencies or capabilities used to drive change. But at companies like IBM, competencies became part of the lexicon—how they made decisions and how they viewed themselves against the competition. They evaluated and rewarded managers based on these criteria, and the criteria provided a common language and way to calibrate talent across the world.

But IBM has gone further still. Over the last several years, Riley and her team have begun to do research on the experiences needed to develop specific competencies for key roles and for *the optimum sequence of those experiences.* "In other words," Riley asks, "can we predict the right steps, the right experiences to develop leaders for certain roles?"

Riley would say that we cannot predict, but we can do a much better job of increasing the odds that they will be successful. At the request of Gerstner, Riley's team set out to better understand the formative experiences for the general manager role at IBM—a tough, challenging job at Big Blue, and one that is difficult to fill. Gerstner identified a core of IBM's best general managers and others he considered less effective. They studied the difference between the two groups and discovered interesting patterns that are now used to guide the development of future general managers at IBM. "We now know that certain experiences early in one's career—accountability for profit and loss, for instance, or an international assignment—are important accelerators," Riley says. They are now looking into other key roles at IBM and replicating the study. "We're not trying to be too mechanical or formulaic," she says. "Human behavior is complex, but we can provide data and information that provide better direction for making key moves."

Internal Audit at The Home Depot

Many functions have developmental initiatives to build functional excellence—rotational assignments for HR, finance, or marketing professionals. They are typically used for early career entrants to learn the lay of the land, to gain a broad perspective of the function, before specializing. The Home Depot's Internal Audit Group, headed by energetic Chuck Pfister with strong support from CFO Carol Tome, has a more ambitious goal: to be a breeding ground for top management.

Modeled after GE's Internal Audit Group, Pfister leads a high-potential group of 80 people—half drawn from inside The Home Depot, the rest from outside. "We feel there's a lot of leverage to be gained if we take bright people, give them intensive training in Six Sigma and other problem-solving and analytical skills, and ask them to work on our toughest problems," says Pfister.

The group had been together less than a year when we spoke, but was organized around the key functional areas of the company. Every four months they rotate through one of four areas where they work on solving critical problems. Two classes of 20 people graduate and replacements are added each year. The top performers from each class are offered advancement opportunities. "We can't think of a better way for people to learn about the entire company and the challenges we face," says Pfister.

Diverse experiences. Challenging assignments. Different leaders and coaches. Rigorous assessments. Feedback-rich environment.

This is how top talent gets better, how they learn how the whole thing works. Another key to the formula is executive education—a time for reflection, a broader perspective, and critically important networking with peers and leaders who teach.

LEADERSHIP EDUCATION

Keswick Hall lies at the foot of the Blue Ridge Mountains east of Charlottesville, Virginia. It is a Tuscan-style villa built in 1912, luxuriously transformed into a grand hotel—Laura Ashley–appointed rooms and 600 acres of lush grounds, including an 18-hole golf course designed by Arnold Palmer. It is an incongruous setting for what's taking place inside.

In a small, dark theater, 25 senior leaders sit transfixed watching a play unfold. A narrator sets the stage.

> In August 1914, the Endurance set sail from Plymouth, England. Their goal was to cross the Antarctic overland. The crew traveled more than 1,000 miles in an open boat crossing the stormiest ocean on earth, and survived an overland trek across forbidding glaciers and over mountains. Led by 40-year-old Sir Ernest Shackleton, the crew faced harrowing adventures. In October 1915, more than a year after they set sail, still half a continent away from their intended base, the ship was trapped and crushed by ice. For the next five months, Shackleton and his men, drifting on ice, were stuck in one of the most dangerous and challenging environments on earth.

The actors appear real. Sound effects and the small, intimate setting add to the drama. At one point, Shackleton leads his imperiled men atop an ice ridge. "I suggest we jump," he says with a calm, firm voice. "Have we any choice?" So they do.

This elaborate stage is the centerpiece for the Executive Leadership Program designed for a technology company's top 200 executives.[6] The play lasts about an hour and is stopped four times for the leaders to discuss the challenges faced by Shackleton. "It is a powerful, emotional setting," says the head of leadership development. "It has had a far more powerful and lasting impact than we ever thought it would. It has become part of our language and a metaphor for the challenges our company faces." The senior vice president of HR says, "It's one thing to lecture employees. It's another to see the issue being played out on stage and almost hear your own words being played out on stage."[7]

This is the CEO's program. He challenged HR and his senior leadership team to provide a forum for emerging leaders to learn, to debate, and to understand. He personally leads a number of the modules and is present the entire four days the program runs. He conducts the program four times a year.

In 1993, 48-year-old Roger Enrico, former chairman and CEO of PepsiCo, contemplated a second career teaching at a university and performing community service. At the same time, Wayne Calloway, then Pepsi's CEO, was concerned that the company's growth was stalled and was at risk because there were too few leaders to drive it. To continue growing at its historical 15 percent rate, Calloway reasoned, the ranks of its key executives would need to swell to 1,500 people in a very short period of time—six or seven years. By his estimate, only 20 percent of the leaders needed resided at PepsiCo at the time.[8] Calloway was determined to convince Enrico, then chairman of PepsiCo's Worldwide Food Division, to stay and teach at PepsiCo.[9]

Enrico was intrigued and set out to design a program that recreated what other senior leaders had done for him. He and other Pepsi executives had grown in an era when a small cadre of executives took young stars under their wings and guided them throughout their careers. Enrico wanted to replicate that experience. He wanted to expand this network of coaches and he wanted to do it in a personal way: small groups—no more than ten people—and every session personally led by him.

Enrico's "Building the Business" program has been given to hundreds of PepsiCo executives. In an 18-month period in the mid-1990s, Enrico ran the program ten times. Like many executive development programs, it included 360-degree feedback assessments, action learning, discussion, debate, and challenge around the company's key strategies. Sessions began at 8:00 A.M. and ran well into the evening, with Enrico leading the way with stories of his successes and failures and what he had learned. He shared how he solved problems, and he pushed participants and sought their opinions and reactions. While many top programs are "owned" by the chief executive, no program has quite the ownership and investment of Enrico's.

Our similar-but-different theme appears more prominent in executive education than almost anywhere else. Companies employ a number of methods to stimulate learning. Theater groups, rope courses, simulations, role playing, and working on real issues and challenges are all part of the arsenal. But there are common themes. We'll briefly discuss three:

- Leaders lead *and teach*.
- Learning and development are tied to critical career stages.
- Action learning is a key methodology.

Leaders Lead and Teach

Andy Grove, the chairman of Intel, believes that training and development is one of the highest-leverage activities a manager can perform.[10] He personally taught new hires—not just senior execu-tives—in boot camp–like sessions, teaching, pushing, and challeng-ing. Jack Welch spent much of his time in Crotonville's pit. Bob Nardelli, Larry Hirsch, A. G. Lafley, and others see their role as building capability, sharing what they know. In describing her role as one of the top leaders at P&G, Melanie Healey says, "If I were to sum it up, it's to live, learn, and pass it on."

This statement characterizes most executive leadership programs at Top Companies. They're often designed by, and certainly almost always led by, senior executives. Eighty-five percent of the programs at GE are conducted by GE leaders. All of P&G's are taught by the company's leaders, its board, or P&G alumni, including a two-day event called Inspirational Leadership led entirely by CEO A. G. Lafley and by the chairman of Saatchi & Saatchi, Kevin Roberts, once an executive at P&G himself.

Having experienced leaders teach has a number of other benefits. Leaders themselves get to hear about concerns and challenges they wouldn't otherwise discover. These leader-teachers also get to hone their own needed skills: how to engage audiences, how to handle tough, challenging questions. And it provides their leaders with yet another look at their talent, which may cause excitement or concern. One executive told us, "I remember a few years ago being in front of a group of our top talent and feeling concerned. There just wasn't enough. So we put into motion a number of programs to turn that around. I am less concerned today."

Learning and Development Are Tied to Career Stages

Education and development at Top Companies are typically de-signed around stages, key milestones in an executive's career. For instance, Top Companies often begin strong with an orientation or onboarding process, knowing that the first few months provide significant opportunities to ground new hires in company values and beliefs. One company offers "Discovery Days"—a three-day event within your first three months where the company provides an overview of all functions and business lines, as well as its expectations for leaders. IBM's "Executive Insights" is an accelerated peek into IBM's complex matrix and culture, as well as its vast array of products and services. Like imprinting, these early moments begin to shape the development and the behaviors Top Companies expect. FedEx's Learning Institute offers three career courses, one at each stage of the management ladder, and participation is mandatory.

Top Companies often sponsor manager workshops; as participants move from manager to executive levels, there are educational workshops or learning series, like IBM's Accelerated Executive Leadership. Later in the executive's career there are more advanced sessions—the Advanced Leadership Services, Parts 1 and 2. These sessions include 360-degree assessments, simulations run by SLG members, and action learning. Each of the executive programs at IBM has an executive sponsor responsible for overall content and delivery.

General Electric's leadership development curriculum centers on six programs, starting with new managers and moving through senior executives:

- Leadership Course (LC)
- New Manager Development Course (NMDC)
- Experienced Manager Course (EMC)
- Manager Development Course (MDC)
- Business Management Course (BMC)
- Executive Development Course (EDC)

As one progresses through these programs, several things happen. The pools from which "students" are drawn become smaller, reflecting GE's hierarchy. Second, as students move through these programs throughout their careers at GE, the instructors increasingly become GE leaders. "Early on, we like to have a mix of insiders and outsiders," says GE's Susan Peters. "As you progress, we focus more and more on *our* challenges, *our* processes, *our* strategies and it's more appropriate for our leaders to lead—and teach."

Action Learning Is a Key Methodology

A key component in nearly all executive education at Top Companies is action learning. Loosely defined, action learning is an intervention that requires action. In some cases, executives are asked to come to the session with a problem or challenge; sometimes the problem is defined in the session itself, and sometimes the business problem or challenge is shaped by senior executives, as in the mission project described in Chapter 3.

At GE and other Top Companies, action-learning assignments are similar to consulting projects. Business unit executives identify critical business issues and challenges and then form the basis for action-learning assignments for key executives. They sometimes study a challenge over a period of months, analyzing data, visiting foreign operations, and understanding market opportunities before presenting their recommendations to division heads.

Action learning has been around for a long time, having its roots in the U.S. military where simulations and problem solving are keys to preparing leaders for conflicts that literally mean life or death. Under the direction of Noel Tichy, the former director of GE's Crotonville facility, GE has taken action learning further than any other company. Tichy and many others believe that adults learn best in conditions of moderate stress, where the stakes are high and meaningful. General Electric will take emerging leaders out of their jobs, divide them into teams, prepare them to address challenging business problems, and assign them a senior executive leader or coach. Assignments can last for months.[11]

Action learning focuses executive students on real challenges, honing skills and capabilities in the workplace, not the classroom. It has the added advantage of allowing a broader set of managers, leaders, coaches, and sponsors to observe, evaluate, and provide feedback on talent they wouldn't otherwise see.

Companies spend $7 billion per year on executive education and almost $14 billion more on managers.[12] But in spite of this enormous expense, leaders at Top Companies keep a balanced perspective about what it provides. It's important, to be sure. It provides perspective, the opportunity to "connect the dots," and can be catalytic in helping executives move to higher levels. It is also the primary vehicle for change initiatives like Six Sigma. Executive education provides the place to strengthen the social network (discussed in Chapter 5) that is so much a part of what Top Companies are all about. "I would say at the end of the day that it's the tail on the dog, it's not the dog itself," says Honeywell CEO David Cote. "If it's not being reinforced through how the company is being run, how the daily activities are working, how decisions get made, then it ends up being just a nice thing."

MAKING SENSE OF IT ALL

In this quick tour across Top Companies, we can see the wide array of approaches used to get the best talent and help them get even better. But in this quick scan, it's still hard to discover what's different, what differentiates the practices of these companies from others. After all, many companies have performance appraisals, some form of talent assessment, promotions, and formal education. But many programs and practices are largely ineffective. At Top Companies there are several overlapping factors that make a difference:

- *Lean design.* Top Companies create processes focused on getting the desired results with the minimum number of steps. Call it the 80/20 rule—it's all about designing processes that contain only the essential steps and information. There is a tendency for the creators of programs and processes to over-build. Top Companies avoid this tendency.

- *Coherence.* Alignment, integration, coherence—choose your word—each works. Programs at Top Companies fit; they are embedded within the business. It feels lean because there are a minimum of moving parts and it's seen as part of the business, how things get done—it's not extra. Discussion of talent is integral to strategy and operations—there's not much of a strategy if you don't have the people to carry it out. To support the business, the programs and practices at Top Companies fit well together and are based on a common framework, set of principles, or competency model. Programs and practices are designed to reinforce the same set of behaviors and are part of a larger, seamless process.

- *Innovation and continuous improvement.* Top Companies are never quite satisfied. No matter how well they do things, they're constantly tinkering, improving on what they do. They unabashedly borrow ideas—not programs—from others and make them their own. They are proud of what they do and can be quite competitive when comparisons are made to others. They believe they are the best. They measure, test, and constantly refine. General Electric's Susan Peters says they regularly scan the environment for new ideas, initiatives to improve. She has a dedicated person focused on reviewing the literature, attending conferences, unabashedly "stealing" ideas and concepts that might work at GE. IBM's Developmental Models and Executive Check-Ins, The Home Depot's Internal Audit Group—these innovative practices don't emerge from a vacuum. They come from measuring, testing, and a constant discomfort in knowing that whatever they do, they still could do it better.

- *Execution*. Former Honeywell CEO Larry Bossidy wrote the book on execution,[13] and leaders at other Top Companies know it to be true—it's all about getting it done. A simple, lean program that is well executed will deliver better results than the flawless program that sits on a shelf. "If you don't know how to execute," says Bossidy, "the whole of your effort as a leader will always be less than the sum of its parts."

  Execution for Top Companies means *focus*—doing those things that matter. It means follow-through and *accountability*. And it means providing appropriate *support* for those focused processes and initiatives, whether that entails using coaches and mentors or enabling technologies that allow processes to run more efficiently.

Lean design, coherence, innovation and continuous improvement, and execution. These are the factors that differentiate the programs and initiatives at Top Companies.

IN SUM

The Gist of It

- Development of leaders of Top Companies is a carefully planned series of experiences focused on those who will most accelerate learning.

- General Electric's Session C, The Home Depot's Strategic Operating and Resource Planning process, and a rigorous selection process ensure that Top Companies differentiate the levels of talent in their organization.

- Formal leadership education is valued, but only when custom-designed for that organization and led by its leaders.

Facts

- Top Companies use experiential development (rotations, global and regional assignments) about 50 percent more frequently than do other companies.

- While many firms design the "right" programs (i.e., 75 percent have formal development processes, 71 percent have succession planning), the Top Companies execute more successfully (91 percent use 360-degree feedback to assess leadership growth, versus 51 percent of other firms).

- Top Companies use succession-planning processes more frequently to actually select leaders for positions.

(continued)

Quote

"It's worth every penny and every minute of time. You can see the return. I know what it costs. I write the checks."

—Carol Tome, CEO, The Home Depot

Consider

- How planned or unplanned are your processes for growing leaders?

- What could you do today to increase the effectiveness of these processes?

- What level of involvement do your company's key leaders have in your leadership development processes?

Notes

1. Much has been written about the leadership pipeline. For more on this, we suggest Noel M. Tichy and Eli Cohen, *The Leadership Engine: How Winning Companies Build Leaders at Every Level* (New York: Harper Business, 1997); Noel M. Tichy and Nancy Cardwell, *The Cycle of Leadership: How Great Leaders Teach Their Companies to Win* (New York: Harper Business, 2002); and Ram Charan, Stephen Drotter, and James Noel, *The Leadership Pipeline: How to Build the Leadership-Powered Company* (San Francisco: Jossey-Bass, 2001).

2. "General Electric Company: The Executive Manpower Operation," Harvard Business School Case Study, 9-680-122, 1980.

3. Louis V. Gerstner, *Who Says Elephants Can't Dance? Inside IBM's Historic Turnaround* (New York: Harper Business, 2002), p. 230.

4. The executive's identity has been disguised at the request of the company.

5. The company's identity has been disguised at the company's own request.

6. The company's identity has been disguised at the company's own request.

7. There are several fascinating books on Shackleton. See the classic by Alfred Lansing, *Endurance: Shackleton's Incredible Voyage* (New York: Carroll & Graf, 1959). There are also several books on the leadership lessons derived from Shackleton's expedition; see, e.g., Margot Morrell and Stephanie Capparrell, *Shackleton's Way: Leadership Lessons from the Great Antarctic Explorer* (New York: Viking, 2001). See also Dennis N. T. Perkins et al., *Leading at the Edge: Leadership Lessons from the Extraordinary Saga of Shackleton's Antarctic Expedition* (New York: Amacom, 2000).

8. See Tichy and Cohen, *The Leadership Engine.*

9. For more on this, see Jay A. Conger and Beth Benjamin, *Building Leaders: How Successful Companies Develop the Next Generation* (San Francisco: Jossey-Bass, 1999).

10. See Thomas J. Neff and James M. Citrin, *Lessons from the Top: In Search of the Best Business Leaders* (London: Penguin Books, 1999).

11. For more on action learning at GE, see Noel M. Tichy and Stratford Sherman, *Control Your Own Destiny or Someone Else Will* (New York: Doubleday, 1993).

12. *Training Magazine,* October 2002.

13. Larry Bossidy, Ram Charan, and Charles Burck, *Execution: The Discipline of Getting Things Done* (New York: Crown Business, 2002).

CHAPTER 5

PAY ATTENTION TO SUBTLETY

THE LITTLE THINGS ARE THE BIG THINGS

When you have done, you have not done for there is more.

—John Donne, 17th-century philosopher

OUR RESEARCH and consulting with Top Companies is conclusive: the three fundamentals—the three truths—count. But even after writing and rewriting these chapters, we felt there was still more. Something was missing. Maybe it's the small, seemingly insignificant patterns that make Top Companies stand out. But our research and experience have led us to discover that the little things *are* the big things. What separates the best companies, the best leaders, the best programs are often nuances, subtleties. It is the combination of little things that amounts to a very *big* difference in organizational life.

Here's what we mean. One of our clients spent some time with one of the Top Companies described in this book to learn what they

---

An early version of this chapter was coauthored with Lauren Cantlon and appeared in *Leader to Leader,* July 2003.

did. He heard about the talent-review process, leadership development, and so on. But he came away unimpressed. "They weren't doing anything different or special. I didn't see it." That's our point. Sometimes it's hard to see, and you certainly won't see it by talking only to HR. We're not knocking HR, but if building great leaders is the job of leaders themselves, then you've got to talk to them—and those they lead—to really see what's going on.

The "little" differences we discovered somehow get lost in the tabulations of practices and programs. Some of this nuance and subtlety is hard to capture in words. The intensity, the feeling, or the collective sixth sense that some leaders or cultures seem to have, an instinct about what matters, cannot be easily conveyed or depicted through words. These leaders don't study what to do, they're the ones studied—it's part of their DNA, it's who they are.

In this chapter we'll attempt to capture some of that subtlety which cuts across all of what we've said so far, and is the extra element that transforms an organization's capabilities to be great at developing leaders. We hope that what's captured here resonates with your experiences and provides you with a glimpse of what we've seen. As one executive we spoke with says, "Paying attention to little things all of the time can be just as important as paying attention to two or three big things a few times."

There are five overlapping ideas that make a big difference:

- It's not just the programs, it's the underlying belief system.
- *How* you communicate is as important as *what* you communicate.
- Taking risks is less risky than not.
- Fostering reciprocity is not equal to an incentive scheme.
- Social networks pave the way.

Each of these five is discussed below.

IT'S NOT JUST THE PROGRAMS, IT'S THE UNDERLYING BELIEF SYSTEM

Leadership isn't just about what leaders do. It's something that they are, which then drives what they do. Genuine leadership comes from within. It's authentic and based on values like honesty, integrity, and trust. Programs and practices are the manifestations of these beliefs and values. They become the embodiment of how leaders believe the enterprise ought to be run. Without this foundation, programs and practices become sterile exercises, lacking in meaning— modern-day bureaucracies that actually lower the credibility of leaders and further disengage associates.

A leader's ability to create and ensure consistency between his or her values matters more than the programs that are in place. The strong personal values of leaders bring life to initiatives; they provide teeth and an in-your-gut feeling that the activities make a meaningful contribution both to individuals and to the organization. Deeply embedded in programs and practices, these values and beliefs provide enduring life that travels through the enterprise and over time; they represent how things are done.

In Chapter 2, we said that CEOs must lead, inspire—provide their stamp, their imprint on talent development. Their drive, focus, and enthusiasm become pervasive—a way of operating that becomes institutionalized. It goes beyond the top executive. Some may label this as "culture," the integrated knowledge, beliefs, and behaviors that are transmitted down to succeeding generations year after year. And although this may be where the consistency begins, we do not believe this is where it ends.

Many of the CEOs we met with are among the most visible and dynamic in the world. They wield enormous power and influence inside and outside the companies they lead. But focusing on them fuels the "cult of personality" arguments that are so prevalent in business and academic circles these days, that great companies are merely shadows of the great leaders who lead them. We think that's a mistaken notion.

Top Companies are not dependent on a single leader. Leadership is institutionalized. It's built into systems, practices, and, yes, the culture. The system of leadership lives beyond the CEO at the helm. Intel has had decades of success under the leadership of Gordon Moore, Andy Grove, and Craig Barrett. Southwest Airlines, under Herb Kelleher and now James Parker. IBM, from Gerstner to Palmisano. General Electric, from Welch to Immelt. Honeywell, from Bossidy to Cote.

There are reasons for these relatively smooth transitions. Sure, there are occasional bumps in the road, but over the long term the leadership at Top Companies will continually renew itself—as Jim O'Toole states, they have high leadership quotients.[1] The process of developing leaders is embedded; it surrounds and permeates the organization.

When we looked for patterns in these belief systems across a number of Top Companies, at least three themes emerged that are institutionalized and become pervasive and evidenced in individual leaders.

Possess an Element of Commitment and Passion to Growing Talent

In Chapter 2, we discussed the focused drive of CEOs and some boards of directors around developing talent and growing leaders. The chief leader must pave the way, set the tone, model the behavior expected of others. The same drive and determination we saw in CEOs at Top Companies was pervasive throughout the management ranks; in fact, the levels of commitment and passion were sometimes even greater. When we asked leaders why they did the things they did to develop leaders, and why they spent 50 to 60 percent of their time doing so, we often received incredulous stares. They either didn't know or couldn't conceive of another way to run an enterprise. To them, these were dumb questions.

One COO we spoke with devotes much of her time and passion to developing future leaders, both informally and formally. Sometimes the more informal situations, she believes, are those that make the biggest impact. She invites young, high-potential employees to travel with her on business trips so they can spend time together, and she can get to know them on a personal level. She also arranges meetings with local high-potential employees when she travels so they have an opportunity to present to her. She gets to see them in action and see how they think. This COO not only believes this is essential, but sees it as fun—there's nothing better than to see people learn and grow and to help them in that process. Ian Cook, executive vice president of Colgate-Palmolive, agrees. "As a leader you have to give of yourself . . . People connect with a number of things and want to emulate a style and set of values and behaviors. Leaders need to take more time and really connect with people."[2]

Many executives at these Top Companies showed a visible increase in their energy level and enthusiasm as they spoke about developing talented employees. Their eyes sparkled, they sat forward in their chairs, and they became more animated and intense. They find working with emerging talent refreshing and energizing and, yes, many described it as fun.

Connect on a Personal Level

A number of years ago, one of us (Robert) was working in manufacturing at a microelectronics plant in Fishkill, New York, for IBM. In the bay for which Robert was responsible, dozens of silicon chips had fallen to the floor. A senior vice president for the division happened to pass by. He pulled Robert aside, put his arm on his shoulders, and started to educate him about the quality and the value of each silicon chip strewn on the floor. Through his patience and line of questioning, he was teaching Robert important lessons. In the coming months, he invested more time educating and developing him.

Across the Top Companies for leaders, we heard numerous stories just like this. Leaders lead—and it's personal. Rod Adkins, general manager of Pervasive Computing at IBM, mentors more than 30 people beyond his own direct reports. He makes a point to spend at least 30 minutes each quarter with each of them. He also initiated a reverse mentoring process, whereby someone who's been with the company less than two years has the opportunity to coach him. He believes that this approach provides him the benefit of learning and receiving feedback from a different perspective, and finds this process personally motivating—and motivating for the younger coaches as well.

Subordinate the Unit for the Greater Whole

In an era when we constantly hear about executive greed, one of the most fascinating—and encouraging—themes that surfaced in a number of our conversations is that of leaders in Top Companies who consistently subordinate their business unit for the good of the larger organization. What leader truly wants to give away great talent once it's identified and nurtured? The answer is, surprisingly, all of them. John Kelly, senior vice president and group executive, Technology Group at IBM, says, "I would give up my best person today if I knew it would serve a group goal . . . I would give him or her up this afternoon." Bob Johnson, CEO of Honeywell Aerospace, reiterated these sentiments. "It's a plus to move people, it's a minus to hoard them . . . and we are keeping score . . . It would be a bad thing for a leader to hold on to a great person . . . it's like priming the pump, when you give up a good leader you'll get another."

As simplistic as these three themes are, they are the critical and differentiating values and principles of the leaders at the Top Companies. These leaders don't think twice about these things; this is the DNA of a well-oiled leadership development philosophy. We heard numerous anecdotes and examples of how these executives use their superior leadership skills to engage and develop future leaders, to foster an effective leadership culture within their organizations. What became increasingly evident as we spoke with these leaders is that they truly believe that if they choose the right people, set the right strategy, provide opportunities, coach, mentor, communicate, and set appropriate long- and short-term stretch goals, the cycle of great leadership will be maintained.

The leaders we spoke with run some of the world's most successful organizations. What makes them so successful is that they recognize that running the business *is* building leadership capability. They have an underlying belief system in the importance and impact of developing leaders that relentlessly shines through time and again.

HOW YOU COMMUNICATE IS AS IMPORTANT AS WHAT YOU COMMUNICATE

Every senior executive everywhere knows that communication is important. Priorities, updates, and target goals need to be reinforced and communicated on a continual and consistent basis. They get it. And in the vast majority of companies, these things do get done, just not well. Too many leaders delegate these tasks to corporate communications specialists who spit out, with great regularity and consistency, messages, themes, and updates to a workforce already numbed by the banality of it all. *The Wall Street Journal* offers more passion and personal connection.

What differentiates the great leaders from the good ones? The innovative and passionate manner in which these essential messages are conveyed. These leaders have an incredible sense of timing; their points are clear, concise, and candid. There's an element of surprise in how they deliver key messages, not always in an outrageous way but just enough to change what's expected, just enough to get the appropriate level of attention. They work hard at simple and repetitive messages—they eliminate corporate-speak. One senior executive reported that when he communicates either in written form or orally, he has a standard test for clarity: "If there are questions as to my intent, I was not clear enough."

Bob Joy, senior vice president of HR at Colgate-Palmolive, claims that Colgate's CEO, Reuben Mark, is the "best communicator" he has ever seen. What is it that Mark does to earn this compliment? "He takes complexity and simplifies it, and he demands this of all of his leaders. He constantly reinforces the importance of focusing on simple but dynamic communication." A senior executive from another company reinforced this point regarding the importance of clear and simple communication: "Communicate, communicate, communicate—very repetitively, very simply—what we are trying to do. We are trying to figure out where we are going. No matter what is happening in the environment, to keep that clear . . . keep a set of high-beam headlights as to where we are going."

One of the important messages that we consistently heard through our interviews was that communication is about more than *what* is said, it's about *how*. It begins at the top of an organization. The CEOs who choose to send out the same predictable communications, to all employees, worldwide, time and again, are not likely to have their messages stick. These sterile, passionless messages, crafted by the corporate communication machine, will not increase engagement among employees or their connection to the company and certainly won't convey a sense of pride, passion, or commitment to the organization. On the other hand, there are the CEOs like the late Sam Walton, founder of Wal-Mart, who declared that if his company hit the numbers, he would do a hula dance on Wall Street. They did, and he did. Herb Kelleher, of Southwest Airlines, created an open and communicative environment at the company through agreeing to do some similarly zany things. Lou Gerstner "invited people to change," and encouraged the employees of IBM to change the way they thought and worked. These leaders practice what they preach and exemplify the art of motivational, committed, and passionate communication, all of which promote a strong leadership culture.

As we described in Chapter 2, leaders at the Top Companies also model or provide visible, tangible support for their priorities. For instance, many leaders struggle trying to empower employees—it promotes innovation, continuous improvement, and quality. There are an endless number of programs, campaigns, themes, and messages on the subject. One CEO implemented the Mission Project, described in Chapter 3, which was an entirely different tactic. He pulled together the two groups of high-potentials and told them, "We don't have all the answers. I want you to go on a discovery mission. I want you to go around the company—all over the world. Talk to people. Talk to our customers. Observe. Discover the two or three things we need to do differently. Report back to the executive team in five months and we'll get them done!" All the communication campaigns you can imagine would not break nearly as much ground as this did. There is just no substitute for such an initiative. "Employees don't want to be ruled," the CEO says, "they want to be involved and to make decisions . . . We don't tell them what to do, we ask them what is right."

TAKING RISKS IS LESS RISKY THAN NOT

The concept of risk taking has existed in organizations for decades in many forms. Product development, innovative marketing, and customer service have all been fertile ground for new approaches that differentiate one company from another. Risk taking at Top Companies, however, is of a different kind. It involves taking their best people and consistently putting them outside their comfort zones. Doing so not only builds capability, but more importantly, builds the necessary confidence to manage more complex leadership roles in the future. Annette Verschuren, division president of The Home Depot's Canadian operations, says, "People have no idea how much capacity they have until you challenge them to higher standards, and they get there."

There are two levels of risk that the Top Companies for developing leaders take. One is at the organizational level—moving the best people across the organization into functional areas or geographies for which they have little experience. But there is also a risk at an individual level, as employees choose to accept opportunities to move out of the comfort zone and into functional areas or geographies for which they have little experience.

Surely, many companies move great talent, but there are differences in how the Top Companies tackle this. For example, Top Companies move their best people with much greater frequency. It was not uncommon for us to hear people talk about having a new position with the organization every 18 to 24 months. Top Companies are also more intentional in the moves they ask people to make. Not only do they have a clearer sense of the competencies and capabilities that emerging leaders need, but they also have more clarity around the experiences that are required for success. And, as we described in Chapter 4, IBM has done so much research on their leaders that they not only know what global and business-unit experiences are needed to develop their leaders, but also can provide optimum sequencing on those moves.

The leaders we spoke with emphasized the importance of taking people and stretching them in a role where they need to develop. "If you keep doing the same thing, you'll likely get pretty good at it, but you're not likely to become a leader," says Mike Lawrie of IBM. "Becoming a leader requires a variety of experiences, honing a number of skills and capabilities, and, as importantly, building confidence along the way." These are risks that some organizations and individuals would not be willing to take, but building great leaders requires that these risks be taken. Another executive believes that risk taking is a big part of his company's great leadership culture. "You talk to many leaders in the company, you know they'll throw out any number of big risks they took . . . some successful, some not. I remember sitting with the CEO and the senior team . . . the CEO looks you in the eyeballs and says, 'If I give you this money, are you going to deliver? And remember, I have a long memory.' That's a serious bet."

The ability and willingness of these organizations to continuously throw opportunities at their employees requires taking chances. These opportunities foster a different kind of learning than any formal education program could possibly address, but developing leaders on the job is risky for both the individual and the institution. What we heard is that this is not just about the risk; it's also about trust and confidence on the part of the organization and the individual. Maria Fernanda Meija, Colgate-Palmolive's general manager in Spain, shared her perspective on this topic when she said, "Once you have common beliefs, it makes it easier to take these risks . . . You understand and accept that moving to New York or Hong Kong is an essential part of what we do and how we run the company."

When presented with such challenges, people often rise to the occasion, knowing that a certain level of trust and confidence in their capability must exist. Realizing your leaders are supporting you can be incredibly motivational. "It's inspiring to know you've been singled out. I wouldn't have picked me for the job," one person told us. "And I wasn't going to let them down." Succeeding also fosters the necessary self-confidence to take further risks and the confidence to take on larger, broader roles. This is, according to one senior vice president and group executive, "the only way to get to the top."

FOSTERING RECIPROCITY IS NOT EQUAL TO AN INCENTIVE SCHEME

According to *Webster's* dictionary, reciprocity is established when there's a "shared feeling on both sides." It implies a "mutual or equivalent exchange or giving back of what has been received." In many leaders' eyes, this sense of giving back is emotional; it is a duty, an obligation to give back more than was given.

"I felt privileged to be singled out—to be moved into key jobs early in my career," one group leader reports. "They sent me to Harvard and to our own executive development programs. My mentors are now running the company. I had the benefit of great coaches. Of course, others in the company were singled out, too. But somehow you were made to feel it was just you, it was personal. It's now my turn to give back."

"I came to this place and never in my wildest dreams did I expect to accomplish what I have," says John Kelly, global head of technology for IBM. "But this company just kept throwing opportunities at me and every time I believe I've got to return their investment in me. I've got to do this for the company and its people." Kelly continues. "The relationship I had with my manager was really special. He took a lot of personal interest, he helped me, coached me, started explaining the company to me, and I didn't understand half a word he was saying, but I guess through osmosis, I absorbed some of that stuff . . . I observed early on that senior people were willing to spend a lot of time with me and take a risk. They didn't have to say it, I sensed this company was different . . . They're going to give this kid out of school the 'jewels to the kingdom'? I took that pretty seriously."

Over and over again we heard executives describe the opportunities given them, the risks their bosses took with them, and the faith and confidence others had—thereby obligating them, solidifying a relationship that no incentive scheme can replicate. There is a key difference between an incentive or reward scheme and the kind of emotional, obligatory sense of responsibility that their reciprocal arrangements bring. Both are effective and both are probably necessary in organizations today. But the latter is more enduring and, in the end, more powerful.

Both are based on an exchange—an exchange of monetary rewards or opportunities for current or future performance. Reward schemes can be motivational and have been shown to change behavior, but the recipient believes he or she has earned what was given. In these reciprocal arrangements, on the other hand, the recipient feels special, "hand picked," not yet deserving of the offer bestowed. In these reciprocal relationships, there is a genuine caring about the whole person, the individual. It is less mechanical than reward systems.

Reciprocity instills a strong sense of pride and desire to give something back to the organization—to foster what was provided for you. One executive we interviewed talked at length about his "responsibility to make sure that the company is optimizing the talent identified to make sure that we are establishing the future technical or management leaders." The leaders we spoke with view their jobs as twofold: to meet a set of financial objectives, and to *build an organization,* not just their own unit, but the larger whole, that can get the job done. There is a sense of pride on the part of the employees that is created in an organization that has developed its leaders, presented them with challenging opportunities, and invested not only time and money in them, but also confidence and trust in their capability to bring the business to the next level. All of this leads to a desire to give back to the organization through building and growing the next generation of great leaders, and a determined spirit that fosters confidence and fortitude throughout the organization.

SOCIAL NETWORKS PAVE THE WAY

There's a critically important by-product of this "movement" of talent—the consistent, regular movement of people across geographies and functions, the deliberate efforts of leaders to spend time with people as they travel, or in executive education forums—and that's the social network that's formed. Leaders should not underestimate the organizational power this brings. One high-potential leader we spoke with said, "We are so network and relationship driven. Networks are a very powerful part of our leadership culture. I would have to start all over again if I were to leave this organization tomorrow . . . As long as I'm here, this network I've acquired follows me."

Social networks pave the way for the belief systems, the communication, the risk taking, and the reciprocity. Through the continuous movement of people and mentoring programs that extend beyond one's own organization, leadership sessions at Crotonville or P&G's "Diaper University," employees have an opportunity to build relationships with people all over the organization. There are a number of benefits. These networks allow great companies to better identify talent—everywhere. Decision making and, more importantly, execution are faster. A common language and framework for tackling problems allow people to quickly move through issues and challenges. Individuals are better able to take pride in accomplishments of the larger enterprise if they have some connections across organizational boundaries—a mentor, a coach, or a sense of connection from having worked in a number of areas. Reflecting on her career this far, one executive says, "The opportunities I've had to work with different teams of people and travel all over the world have allowed me to create a strong network of friends and colleagues . . . we all continue to support each other."

One executive, talking about the programs at his company, says, "Very early on leaders meet their peers, spend time with them in both formal and informal forums, and have the opportunity to build a rapport with this group of people. This is as important as the [leadership development] classes themselves." Lois Juliber talked about similar experiences and opportunities at Colgate-Palmolive through leadership development classes that expose high-potentials both to their peers and to senior executives. Through leadership training programs, moving around within the organization, and meeting peers and mentors in both informal and formal venues, these social networks are created and shape the relationships that employees have throughout their careers. "We all know each other," one executive notes. "What differentiates this organization is a tremendous sense of global cohesiveness."

General Electric has more than 300,000 employees—13 businesses in wide-ranging industries from aircraft engines to light bulbs to financial services. It could be a highly fragmented, difficult-to-navigate operation. Its performance-driven culture could breed internal competition, the hoarding of ideas and people. General Electric is not this way at all.

Instead, GE is remarkably informal—and connected. The company fosters communities of practices—functional alignments across business units, Crotonville, special task forces, project teams, and the movement of talent within and across business units. "If you're here long enough," says one GE executive, "it's amazing how many of our 300,000 people you know." Pay and promotions are tied to "boundaryless behavior." Six Sigma and Workout, Session C, and operating and budget reviews are common processes across GE, creating a single vernacular and way of looking at the world of business. It's unlikely that there's another company as successful that is open to ideas—from anywhere—and there's certainly no company its size that can implement ideas as quickly. In 1999, a GE Capital manager in London told Jack Welch that younger employees were teaching older executives how to use the Internet. Within a few days, Welch issued an edict that every senior manager—himself included—would find an Internet mentor.[3]

Ultimately, the little things are the big things. Beliefs and behaviors of individuals form patterns in these organizations. These little things become institutionalized. Leaders experience what was done for them. They observe. They perpetuate a system, a culture, and the network allows it to travel through time and across boundaries. It is powerful and enduring. It is cultural and, indeed, difficult to replicate through the mechanical application of practices. Through a strong belief system and values that support strong leadership development, these organizations have ensured a legacy of developing and encouraging the growth of great leaders long after their current leaders are gone. They have ingrained these processes and mindsets into the next generation, enabling the leadership culture to continue indefinitely. In the end, as one leader told us, "ya gotta believe."

IN SUM

The Gist of It

- The three leadership Truths provide companies with the critical foundation needed to build strong leaders. Even with these pieces in place, however, their ultimate success may also depend on effectively managing the more subtle aspects of the process. We recommend that leaders pay attention to five "Little Things" when trying to build great leaders:

- The underlying belief system, not just the programs

- Communicating: *How* is as important as *what*

- Taking risks is less risky than not

- Fostering reciprocity

- Paving the way with social networks

Quotes

"If there are questions as to my intent, I was not clear enough."

—*a senior executive*

"Employees don't want to be ruled; they want to be involved and to make decisions . . . We don't tell them what to do, we ask them what is right . . ."

—*a CEO*

Consider

- What are the few subtle factors that (will) allow your leadership practices to be successful?

Notes

1. See, e.g., James O'Toole, "When Leadership Is an Organizational Trait," in *The Future of Leadership: Today's Top Thinkers Speak to Tomorrow's Leaders,* ed. Warren Bennis, Gretchen M. Spreitzer, and Thomas G. Cummings (San Francisco: Jossey-Bass, 2001), pp. 158–174.

2. Lou Gerstner and others have made this point; see Louis V. Gerstner, *Who Says Elephants Can't Dance? Inside IBM's Historic Turnaround* (New York: Harper Business, 2002).

3. John Micklethwait and Adrian Wooldrige, *A Future Perfect: The Challenge and Promise of Globalization* (New York: Random House, 2003).

CHAPTER 6

STARTING FROM SCRATCH TO BUILD A STRONG LEADERSHIP PIPELINE

A good beginning makes a good end.

—*English Proverb*

ALL SUCCESSFUL programs and initiatives for developing leadership talent are implemented to support important business needs. They are sustained and viable only to the extent that they continue to meet those business needs. These programs are not in place just to imitate what best companies do. If that's the case, they will fail or have only modest impact. Only when processes and initiatives are an integral part of running the business—fueling growth, ensuring the human capital and leadership needs are fulfilled—will they succeed.

In this chapter, we begin a slight shift from what we learned about Top Companies to helping you apply these learnings in your organization. Many people are uncertain where to begin; others argue themselves into inaction by claiming "we're not GE" or "we don't have Lou Gerstner," or "they've been doing that for years—show me a company that started from scratch." Still others take a deep dive, launching initiatives, devising often expensive leadership development programs loaded with big-name speakers, but with no real plan for building a sustainable system.

Many of the companies described in this book had different starting points—some had very little in place to identify and develop leaders. Some had to transform antiquated and disjointed systems and processes. Under the direct hand of Pepsi's former CEO Roger Enrico, the consumer products giant upended their approach to developing leaders, a process further enhanced by new Pepsi CEO Steve Reinemund. Until a few short years ago, Colgate-Palmolive had a basic and fragmented process for developing leaders. The Home Depot had virtually no infrastructure to support a $46 billion company. Under CEO A. G. Lafley and global HR officer Dick Antoine, P&G has injected new life and discipline to support an aggressive growth strategy. Even those with strong programs and history—like GE and IBM—are constantly improving, measuring, and modifying what they do. They avoid resting on their laurels. The Home Depot's CEO Bob Nardelli says, "I'm not sure we can ever do enough to ensure the biggest variable we have—the associate—is prepared . . . Success breeds complacency, complacency leads to arrogance, and arrogance to failure."

The following pages provide you with a starting point—a place to begin. We introduce several frameworks for building a leadership strategy that makes sense for your company. We provide examples and models drawn from Top Companies and our consulting experiences that will help you pinpoint the leverage and focus on what you need to start strong. Additional tools, questions, and checklists to support change initiatives in your organization can be found in the Toolkit in Appendix B. The approaches we describe are practical and pragmatic, giving both line managers and HR executives the support they need to start building a great company for leaders.

Since everything in leadership begins and ends with the business, we start there.

The Business Context First

When Lou Gerstner took over IBM in 1993, he took action to stem the company's mounting financial losses. He restructured the business to support a change in strategy—a move to a more integrated, network-centric enterprise that focused more on services than on hardware (IBM's historical strength). He laid off tens of thousands of employees. And *he focused his attention on Big Blue's leadership talent.* He instinctively knew that without the right people in place, he'd be unable to turn the enterprise around or draw the talent needed at entry levels to sustain IBM over the long term.

In Gerstner's first few years, over half of IBM's top 300 executives were gone. It's not that they were bad people or incompetent, they simply were not what the company needed at that time.

When Bob Nardelli became CEO at The Home Depot, he accelerated the company's growth strategy. The Home Depot now opens a new store every 43 hours. They hire 40,000 new associates every year to fill roles that did not exist before; they hire another 60,000 to replace employees who leave, something Nardelli and his chief HR officer, Dennis Donovan, are trying hard to reduce. *Where will they get the leadership needed to support that growth?* "Leadership has been and will be the key differentiator for any company," says Nardelli. "The biggest dependent factor we have at The Home Depot is our associates—and the biggest *variability* is our associates," he says. "Every day, 300,000 associates strap on an orange apron. They're involved in 1.2 billion register transactions per year. If those customers do not have a positive experience, they won't come back. There is no insignificant transaction by any associate here. They are our brand. And if those associates do not have a positive employment experience, they won't come back, either. Leadership is the key for both."

Nardelli and Donovan back up their words. The Home Depot will provide 19 million hours of training this year and they'll spend over $4 billion developing talent. In the six months prior to our meeting with him, Nardelli had been in front of every one of the company's nearly 2,000 managers not once, but twice. They have instituted the Strategic Operating and Resource (SOAR) review process (described in Chapter 4), providing an integrated approach to running the business. SOAR, which includes a rigorous talent review, is being used down to the store level.

"The Home Depot is a great company," says Donovan. "But what we did to get us to $46 billion in sales will not get us to $100 billion," he says. "We had no infrastructure—no system or process to get us to the next level."

Strong leaders have always understood the senior executive group is the place to begin when changing direction. General Electric's revered Crotonville in Ossining, New York, was built in the mid-to-late 1950s by then-CEO Ralph Cordiner. Cordiner orchestrated a dramatic transformation of GE. He fundamentally changed the structure of the modern enterprise. He broke down company activities into 20 operating divisions and 70 departments. Cordiner's reorganization went further than any other at the time—or since—and the aggressive decentralization propelled GE into nuclear power, jets, computers, and industrial automation systems.[1]

The decentralization model still exists in GE today. But in the 1950s, it was a dramatic break from the past. Cordiner built Crotonville to prepare managers and leaders to operate in a new, innovative, decentralized world. Tens of thousands of GE managers were taught how to manage their own operations with profit and loss responsibility. But when Jack Welch took over GE in 1981, Crotonville had grown tired. The facilities had aged; its courses—and instructors—had lost their vitality. It was no longer integral to the business. It was a tangent.

Walter Wriston, former chairman of Citibank and long-time board member at GE, once told Welch that as chairman and CEO, he would be the last to know when anything is going on in the company. Welch was determined to prove him wrong. Crotonville—and Session C—allowed him to do that.[2]

Welch embarked on a change that set into motion a holistic approach to leadership at GE that also became a model for companies throughout the world. He wanted a place to spread ideas, to directly connect with managers, to challenge and debate. "I wanted to change everything: the students, the faculty, the content, and the physical appearance of the facilities," Welch says. "I wanted it to be a place to reach the hearts and minds of the Company's best people—the inspirational glue that holds things together as we changed," he says of his vision. "I don't want anyone to go there who doesn't have great potential. I want the good ones coming up, not the tired ones looking for a last reward."[3]

With that, GE began building its now legendary programs. Investments were substantial, but Welch knew the payoff. Crotonville became the metaphor for Welch's sweeping transformation across GE. He renovated the now famous "Pit," the main multilevel classroom, built a helipad so GE's leaders could be easily transported from corporate headquarters in Fairfield, Connecticut, an hour's drive away. When then center director, Jim Boughman, the former Harvard Business School professor, pitched a new $46 million residence center, Welch reviewed his presentation and payback analysis. Welch drew an "X" through the return-on-investment page and scrawled the word *Infinite*. He felt the returns on GE's investment would last forever. And he meant it.

Crotonville has been called GE's glue, but too many companies attempt to mimic GE by building elaborate campuses or leadership development programs in isolation of anything else. They fail to recognize that Crotonville is only a part of a much larger system—rigorous talent selection, Session C, 360-degree feedback, Noel Tichy-inspired action learning, and strong differentiation of talent focusing on both results and leadership behaviors. Managing talent and developing leaders at GE has become institutionalized. It is the way they run the business. It is embedded. It is no longer a tangent.

These examples highlight a basic theme throughout this book: Great leadership programs are not programs at all. They are essential processes for driving the business.

Defining What You Need—creating a Business Strategy—leadership Strategy Link

We've spoken with dozens of executives about their careers—the milestones, the turning points, the influences. In some cases, formative events were accidental, fortuitous situations that provided real learning or challenge that could not have been planned. In many cases, career moves sounded almost like a grand master moving the chess pieces around the board—careful moves at exactly the right time to build the skills and the confidence to become a great leader.

The truth, of course, lies somewhere in between. Now presiding over large, complex enterprises, leaders ask the fundamental questions that are—or should be—at the heart of any process or system to build leadership capability: *What do we need? What kind of leader excels here today? What kind of leaders will be needed for tomorrow? How and where do we get them?* The answers to these questions form the foundation of a company's leadership strategy.

A leadership strategy describes how you will support your business strategy. We suggest focusing on four levers: *selecting, developing, assessing,* and *compensating* your leaders. It should be as fundamental a part of running the business as a manufacturing or financial strategy. Ultimately, how you use these four levers will dictate the type of leaders that will be attracted to and retained by your organization.

Companies with strong leadership strategies have carefully planned each of those areas so they both support the business strategy and integrate with the other leadership tactics.

We'll return to the four levers later in this chapter and in Appendix B, but first we want to discuss tightening the line to your business strategy.

STARTING WITH CRITICAL CAPABILITIES

Crafting your leadership strategy starts with identifying the critical capabilities your leaders will need to realize your long-term business goals. Looking across the landscape of companies, capability or competency models are more similar than different. At one level, this is to be expected. Leadership is leadership. *How different do we expect the attributes to be across companies?*

At another level, we would expect at least some differences to emerge. Organizations are different—there are differences in core capabilities, ways of operating, history, culture, and beliefs about how to manage and lead. We would expect these differences to emerge in the development of the competency model. Most importantly, if competencies serve to differentiate the quality of your leaders, then the behaviors should reflect the unique challenges faced by your organization.

Executives and managers frequently complain, too, that competency models are often too abstract, too general, to drive action or provide the specificity needed to make selection decisions. This is not to say it shouldn't be done. Sometimes the journey alone is worth the effort. A good process allows executive teams to challenge and debate what's needed, to refine their thinking, and to calibrate among themselves what it takes to lead. But it's also important to keep these models in perspective. It's a starting place for dialogue and discussion about what's needed, an attempt to add clarity about expectations. Some firms take this too far and attempt to explicitly define leaders' behaviors with 10, 30, or even 50 different requirements. We suggest that instead you focus on the vital few behaviors that will define success, much like Gerstner did at IBM.

Arriving at these vital few can be a challenging process, but there's a tremendous payoff from a more disciplined approach that identifies the few differentiating leadership characteristics. Selecting those three, four, or five truly defining competencies provides leaders in your organization with clarity about what's really important, simplifies the review of performance against those behaviors, and focuses coaching and development on building the organization's unique strengths. Getting there is less complicated than you might imagine.

THE STRATEGIC LEADERSHIP MATRIX

At Hewitt, we use the Strategic Leadership Matrix (SLM; see Figure 6.1) with our clients to help identify the vital few capabilities needed by their leaders. The SLM combines two critical dimensions—the amount of change facing the business, and the degree of growth or return in a company's strategy—to understand the type of leaders and leadership systems needed in a business. It relies on a wealth of research and the intuitive concept that a leader's performance will increase as the fit between the leader and his or her role increases.

This concept of "fit" can be defined in a number of different ways, but our experience has shown that two factors capture most of what defines how well a leader fits with his or her role: the business strategy and the amount of change in the environment. This means that, contrary to some of the claims being made by many consultants and academics, there is no universal best-leader model that describes the ideal leadership characteristics for every situation. While some core

Figure 6.1
Strategic Leadership Matrix (SLM)

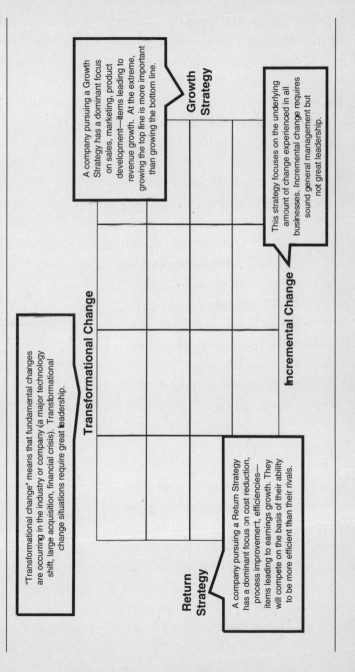

"Transformational change" means that fundamental changes are occurring in the industry or company (a major technology shift, large acquisition, financial crisis). Transformational change situations require great leadership.

Transformational Change

A company pursuing a Growth Strategy has a dominant focus on sales, marketing, product development—items leading to revenue growth. At the extreme, growing the top line is more important than growing the bottom line.

Growth Strategy

This strategy focuses on the underlying amount of change experienced in all businesses. Incremental change requires sound general management but not great leadership.

Incremental Change

Return Strategy

A company pursuing a Return Strategy has a dominant focus on cost reduction, process improvement, efficiencies—items leading to earnings growth. They will compete on the basis of their ability to be more efficient than their rivals.

behaviors—high ethical and moral standards, strong communication skills, and a belief in the power of people, among others—are essential in all great leaders, none of these describes specifically what a leader needs to realize *your* business strategy.

Before we explain how to select your vital few competencies using the SLM, we should clarify a few quick definitions.

RETURN STRATEGY VERSUS GROWTH STRATEGY

There are many types of business strategies, and great strategy authors like Porter, Slywotzky, and Prahalad[4] have classified them under a variety of labels from "Value Migration" to "Core Competencies." While not judging the efficacy of any of those models, we believe that any business strategy can be simplified so that it's represented on a continuum from "primarily seeking growth" to "primarily seeking financial return." From a leadership perspective, we're not concerned with your actual strategy choice, just that you have the right leadership strategy to support it.

Growth Strategy

A growth strategy is primarily focused on revenue growth. It's likely that marketing, sales, new products, and innovation are already hallmarks of your company. You believe that a focus on aggressively growing the top line is the key to continued corporate success. While you may also strive to have efficient manufacturing processes or implement Six Sigma, these are not your bases for competing. Defining yourself as having a growth strategy doesn't mean you aren't pursuing profits; you just plan to achieve them primarily by expanding sales, not primarily through being the lowest-cost operator (and, conversely, a return strategy doesn't mean you aren't pursuing growth).

One example of a strong growth strategy was Amazon.com in the 1990s. One of the earliest entrants to online retailing, Amazon focused on aggressively growing the top line (revenues) of the business. From 1995 to 2002, Amazon posted a cumulative net loss of $3 billion, in one of the longest streaks of unprofitability of any company in history. But at the same time, its annual revenues increased from $511,000 to nearly $4 billion dollars. This gave them the funding necessary to continue building the business to the size necessary for efficiency and eventual profitability.

During that period, Amazon valued a dollar of top-line growth over a dollar of bottom-line growth. Why? Because even if you're losing 20¢ on every $1 of product sold, a $4 billion revenue stream can fund much more expansion than a $40 million one. That additional investment can then later pay off any debt built during that period of time (or deliver earnings that appeal to the stock market so shareholders benefit). Amazon's leader then and today, Jeff Bezos, can be described as the ultimate growth leader.

Return Strategy

A return strategy says that cost reduction, efficiencies, and process improvements are the heart of your competitive strategy. A large part of your corporate resources is likely devoted to ensuring you are the most efficient provider of goods or services. While you may intend to grow while executing your strategy, you will compete on the basis of having a more efficient organization than your competitors.

Wal-Mart is a great example of a firm with a return strategy. One of the most successful firms of the last 40 years, Wal-Mart's legendary focus on cost control secured ownership of a marketplace formerly dominated by K-Mart, Woolworth, and a few other firms that competed primarily on price. Wal-Mart has grown fivefold in the past ten years, from $55 billion in sales in 1993 to $244 billion in 2003. During that same period, Woolworth disappeared from the marketplace and K-Mart went through a wrenching bankruptcy, largely brought on by a failed attempt to mirror Wal-Mart's low-price strategy.

While Wal-Mart was one of the fastest-growing companies of the 1990s, their strategic choice for competition was to be the low-cost provider of products and services. They made significant investments in novel logistics arrangements, including direct electronic links between individual store inventories and their major suppliers to facilitate reordering. This type of improvement was grounded in reducing inventory costs and product shortages so they could be the lowest-cost provider of goods and services. Their strategy clearly falls into the "return" category.

It's unlikely that a successful leader at "growth"-focused Amazon.com would be a successful leader at the "return" leader Wal-Mart—the fit just wouldn't be there. Similarly, the successful "return" leader probably isn't interested in working in a fast-growing start-up. A good leadership strategy acknowledges this and tries to closely match leaders with the company environment.

TRANSACTIONAL VERSUS TRANSFORMATIONAL CHANGE

The other key dimension of leadership fit involves the degree of change an organization will experience during the next few years. We measure this on a scale ranging from "transactional" to "transformational."

Transactional Change

While most companies today face a challenging business environment, this new pace of change has become expected, in contrast to the greater predictability of years past. This doesn't ignore that the business environment is always changing and that leaders will be faced with new challenges daily. It just defines this as the bottom of the scale relative to transformational change. We call this underlying level of change experienced by all businesses "transactional change" and believe that most leaders are able to manage this level of challenge with relative ease.

Transformational Change

Other firms are undergoing more dramatic change—large acquisitions, industry transformations, or financial crises—or "transformational change."[5] These companies need leaders who can guide the company through turbulent times, leaders with a strong vision, great communication capabilities, charisma, and other characteristics that instill confidence in followers. Other companies may need what leadership scholar Jim O'Toole calls "yellow light leaders"[6]—individuals who are effective midway between the transactional and transformational views. In either case, these leaders are capable of, and interested in, steering a company through more turbulence than many of their peers are.

Similar to leaders' fit with a business strategy, leaders need to be comfortable with, and capable of dealing with, different degrees of change. Those who thrive on new situations and enjoy uncertainty and ambiguity will be closer to the transformational end of the spectrum. Those who prefer less drama in their daily work will likely fit best at the transactional end.

Your placement on the SLM defines the types of leaders that are best suited to lead your company in the future and the competencies that are required for them and the business to succeed. There are specific competencies associated with where you place on this matrix (see Figure 6.2) and if your leaders don't possess those capabilities, we believe your corporate performance will suffer. It is through an exercise like this that you should define the competencies required by your leaders, focusing on those items that will truly differentiate your organization. We're often asked if this approach means that a company should have a new competency model every time its strategy changes. We would say that the competencies should always reflect your business strategy at least two to three years out. If this means that every few years you need to modify these competencies, so be it. The key is to explain to your leaders why you're shifting what's required of them and how you'll help them engage in these new behaviors.

Again, this process makes no judgment about the *correctness* of a strategic choice. If your firm has made a bad strategy decision, aligning your leaders with the capabilities needed to execute that strategy will simply get you to the wrong outcome even faster.

The degree of change is an important consideration for other reasons as well—it tells you how quickly you need to act. If you see your organization heading toward a calmer, return mode and you've just come from a period of rapid growth (or vice versa), it's likely that you haven't built the capabilities you need to succeed in that new environment. Removing people in critical positions and replacing them with leadership talent and skill for new business models is often necessary while concurrently building and developing less-experienced talent over the long term. This doesn't mean that you need to fire your current leaders and hire a completely fresh set. But it does mean that in every key function you wish to change, the senior leader must be someone who either embodies, or can quickly adapt to, the critical behaviors identified for success.

The degree of change often defines the mix of insiders versus out-

Figure 6.2
Representative Capabilities for Each Scenario

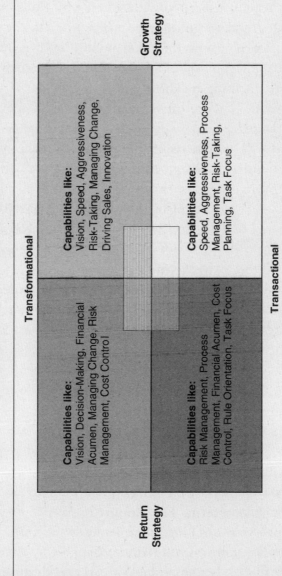

siders. It is not simply a philosophical discussion about what is *desired*. It's often driven by what you *need* and the urgency around that need. Many CEOs told us they want to build the system, the pipeline, to substantially reduce the number of outside hires, but business conditions—the rate of change, a redirection of strategy—preclude them from doing so. They simply can't grow enough of the right people fast enough.

As an example, a recent client of ours—let's call them ABC Utility—was moving from a regulated to a deregulated environment, a change requiring a fundamental shift in how the firm managed many parts of its business. In a regulated environment, its strategy was to ensure a consistent rate of return for stockholders by controlling the cost of raw materials and other general and administrative expenses. Government regulators set the fees they could charge and the customers they could serve, so top-line revenue growth was much more challenging than increasing profit margins by controlling costs. The speed and pace of change was modest. Valuable leaders, in that environment, were skilled in Six Sigma, process management, and operational efficiency. There was little need for transformational capabilities—good managerial skills sufficed. On the Strategic Leadership Matrix, ABC would be in the lower left corner (see Figure 6.3) and the capabilities that specifically matched that business would be relatively unique to this position.

Deregulation presented a fundamentally different challenge for ABC Utility. They were free to sell power to virtually any consumer, at the prevailing market rates or through futures contracts. New markets opened, and sales and marketing techniques had to be put in place to attract consumers. Competitors moved in to steal the most profitable customers. Investors expected rates of return at least competitive with those of other utilities. Employees, not used to these competitive pressures, had to respond with nimbleness and flexibility they had not experienced before. It was a different world and required different leaders.

Figure 6.3
Strategic Leadership Matrix: Change Scenario

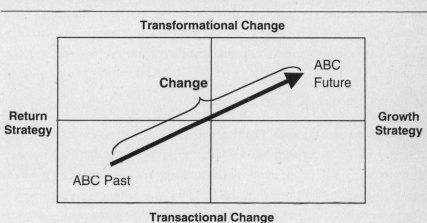

On the Strategic Leadership Matrix, the new ABC was high on change and focused on growth—the upper right quadrant. This transformational growth leader needed to focus on marketing, sales, the end customer, and innovation—the hallmarks of a growing business.

ABC Utility recognized that the leaders who had served the company well in its regulated days could not lead it going forward. The capabilities, experience, and mindset were fundamentally different from what was required in the past and they didn't have the luxury of time to develop leaders for this challenge. Instead they recruited leaders into top positions from companies that had either undergone a similar change or were strongly oriented toward growth. ABC is now filling in behind these senior hires with a more appropriate recruiting and development strategy for this more dynamic environment.

Through an exercise like the SLM, you can identify the vital few capabilities and behaviors you need from future leaders. But defining these capabilities is only the first step. To actually grow and reinforce these capabilities you must ensure that your leadership systems—how you source, develop, align, and reward your leaders—actually promote their growth. It's a task easier said than done, but one that's made easier if you understand how each of the various systems in your organization contributes to competency development.

Measurement and Accountability

Top Companies succeed at building great leaders for each of the reasons described in this chapter, but also for a more fundamental one—they hold current leaders accountable for building the next generation of leadership. Our 2003 Top Companies for Leaders survey showed that 95 percent of the U.S. Top Companies hold leaders accountable. Only 43 percent of the other organizations that participated made a similar claim. Holding leaders accountable for building leadership capability seems to differentiate better performing organizations from their lower performing peers. Among companies performing in the 75th percentile or higher for Return on Equity (ROE), 42 percent hold leaders accountable for developing leadership capability compared to only 3 percent of companies below the 25th percentile for ROE.

Holding leaders accountable for developing their teams doesn't need to be a complicated process, but it does require that a few fundamental building blocks be in place. CEOs need to support the use of this measure and give it sufficient weight in the process to attract leaders' attention. Companies like PepsiCo weight developing others as 30 percent of the leader's bonus opportunity. Leaders also need to understand what tools and processes are available to help them achieve this goal, and what metrics will be used to measure their performance against it. All organizations should implement these fundamental steps; they are a simple but powerful tool to fill the leadership pipeline.

FROM STRATEGY TO TACTICS: MAKING IT REAL

Organizations have many levers to reinforce the right behaviors and ensure they have the capabilities needed for success. They can hire and promote different leaders, and they can use performance management, rewards, communication, and engagement tactics to reinforce certain messages, values, and priorities. They can develop critical skills through assignments, coaching, and mentoring. Ideally, the practices in each of these areas reinforce the same set of behaviors and are well integrated (i.e., performance management seamlessly flows into succession planning). We use the Leadership LifeCycle™ (see Figure 6.4) as an easy way to understand the levers in each area and to ensure they fit together.

Where to Start

The SLM provides the initial framework for defining the capabilities and behaviors needed from your leaders. Using this framework helps identify key gaps between what you have and what you need. The Leadership LifeCycle—source, align, develop, and reward—provides structure for assessing and closing the gaps.

- *Sourcing.* How you will obtain the leaders you need to meet your business goals. This includes the balance between making leaders (developing them internally) or buying them (recruiting externally) and the processes for doing each. At a practical level, it includes succession planning, search-firm relationships, and building a leadership brand, among others.
- *Aligning.* How you will ensure leaders are aligned with business goals and engaged with their jobs. "Alignment" refers to how well you're building expectations with leaders, what

Figure 6.4
Leadership LifeCycle™

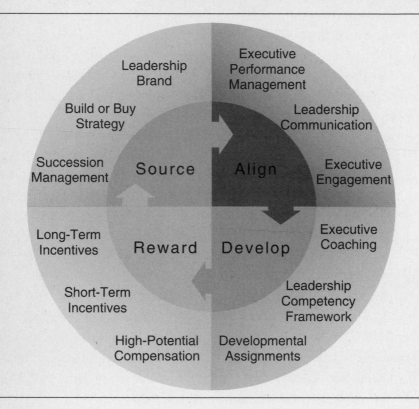

business results they're expected to accomplish, and how well you've built a leadership environment that fully engages leaders with the challenges you've established for them.

- *Developing.* How you will build the capabilities, knowledge, and self-awareness of your leaders. This includes the assignment–matching process that should flow from succession planning, to executive coaching, to mentoring, to any formal development programs.

- *Rewarding.* How you will compensate leaders to drive performance, reward success, and differentiate high performers. Rewarding would include base pay, annual incentives, and
  long-term incentives.

Once you understand your leadership requirements from the
SLM, consider the implications of each of these areas on your leadership practices. Are your current practices aligned with the business
strategy that you plan to achieve? Which practices provide the most
leverage and which need to be realigned? Most importantly, do the
pieces mutually reinforce each other, sending consistent messages
about the behaviors that you'll encourage and reward?

Revisiting our case study company, ABC Utility, an overview of
their leadership strategy for their new environment might look
like Table 6.1. We included more specific tools in the Toolkit in
Appendix B at the end of the book, which we've organized around
the three leadership Truths—CEO and Board Leadership and Inspiration, Maniacal Focus on the Best Talent, and The Right Programs Done Right—to make getting started on the right things a
bit easier.

While starting from scratch isn't easy, it can be done—all of our
Top Companies were there at one time. In many cases it's actually
easier to start from scratch since there are fewer bad programs and
processes to dismantle first. As you start designing these practices,
keep your business strategy as your ultimate guide, regularly asking
yourself, *"How will this specifically help us achieve our business objectives?"*
and *"Does this practice give us the best return on our investment in building
leaders?"* You likely won't get it completely right on the first try, but
if you have in place a robust, systemic approach to growing leadership quality and depth, you'll be far ahead of many of your competitors. And before you start, ensure that you have a CEO who will be
a passionate, involved sponsor of the process you intend to build.

Table 6.1
Sample Leadership Strategy
Summary: ABC Utility

Critical Competencies

We've identified the following five competencies as most important for our executives given our business strategy and our change environment:

- Grows the business
- Drives change
- Builds commitment
- Maximizes talent quality
- Focuses on the customer

Sourcing Leaders

- *Make/buy mix.* We will balance the ratio of internal hires/external hires in leadership at 70/30 to encourage new ideas and challenge our culture while providing opportunities for internal development.
- *Succession planning.* Our succession-planning process will be the exclusive method for placing leaders into jobs. We will identify candidates and match them with opportunities based on this process, using the competencies as a primary screen.
- *Onboarding leaders.* Retention and success of leaders in new roles (from inside or outside the company) will be increased through a process that provides guidance and coaching around both personal performance and relationship building.

Aligning Leaders

- *Performance management.* We will set aggressive goals for all leaders in our performance management process, ensuring that stretch goals are a key component and that a balanced measurement of business performance and individual behaviors occurs.
- *Engaging leaders.* Executive engagement will be actively monitored through yearly surveys with HR and the executive team held jointly accountable for identifying and improving deficiencies.
- *Executive coaching.* Providing select executives with coaching to further performance will be a core aspect of our strategy.

Table 6.1
Continued

Developing Leaders

- *Assignment-based development.* Job assignments will be the primary method for developing leaders, and a process to match individuals and jobs will flow from succession planning. Support of internal coaches will be provided to leaders in developmental assignments to help ensure success.
- *High-potential development.* Our highest-potential employees will receive a disproportionate share of developmental resources. We will develop group activities for them, increase their exposure to the senior team and board, and review their performance on a semi-annual basis.
- *Executive development.* We will provide group-based sessions for our leaders to develop capabilities in serving customers and communicating a clear vision and business acumen.

Rewarding Leaders

- *Base pay.* We will set the 50th percentile as the goal for base pay, with high-potential employees identified through our succession process being paid at the 60th percentile.
- *Annual incentive.* We will provide a 75th percentile target for annual incentive, strongly differentiating between median performers and high performers in distributing rewards.
- *Long-term incentives.* We will use a combination of performance-vesting stock and regular stock options to provide incentives for consistent leader behavior. We will target the 75th percentile for these awards, strongly differentiating between median performers and high performers.

Finding and developing leaders will become more challenging in the future than it is today. Companies that do this well will clearly stand out and enjoy a significant competitive advantage over others. Those companies investing the time to design great practices and the dedication of resources will stand a much better chance of having the leaders they need to grow the business, respond to unexpected challenges, and effectively lead employees through change. Those without a systemic approach will take their chance in the free market, opportunistically hiring leaders if they can find them, and will likely fail or enjoy modest, short-term success.

The future poses new challenges and greater speed and complexity, but also opportunities to develop leadership capability more effectively. We'll discuss each of these in more detail in Chapter 7. The future Top Companies will be those that recognize these new challenges early and respond aggressively, relying on a foundation of senior team support, a maniacal focus on their best talent, and doing the right programs the right way.

IN SUM

The Gist of It

- Leadership processes should link directly to the business strategy, supporting its achievement by selecting, aligning, developing, and rewarding leaders to act consistently with that strategy.

- Leaders who fit with the business will drive higher performance for the organization. We define "fit" using two criteria: the business strategy (measured on a continuum from a growth strategy to a return strategy) and the change environment (measured on a continuum from incremental change to transformational change). Identifying where your company falls on these two dimensions provides strong direction about the types of leaders needed.

- Companies starting from scratch or interested in assessing their current capabilities can use the Leadership LifeCycle™ to understand the levers they can use to reinforce leadership behaviors.

(continued)

Facts

- Top Companies use developmental practices more frequently than other companies, but in a way that's aligned with their specific business needs.

Quote

"The Home Depot is a great company, but what we did to get us to $46 billion in sales will not get us to $100 billion. We had no infrastructure—no system or process to get us to the next level."

—Dennis Donovan, senior vice president of HR, The Home Depot

Consider

- What broad implications does your business strategy have on your leadership needs?

- What are the capabilities that will define the successful leaders in your company in two to four years?

- How effectively do your current leadership practices reinforce the behaviors you feel are most critical?

NOTES

1. Alfred D. Chandler, Jr., *Strategy and Structure: Chapters in the History of the American Industrial Enterprise* (Cambridge: MIT Press, 1962).

2. Robert Slater, *Jack Welch and the GE Way: Management Insights and Leadership Secrets of the Legendary CEO* (New York: McGraw-Hill, 1999).

3. Jack Welch (with John A. Byrne), *Jack: Straight from the Gut* (New York: Warner Books, 2001), p. 171.

4. These are among many great strategy models available: Michael Porter, *Competitive Strategy* (New York: Free Press, 1998); Gary Hamel and C. K. Prahalad, *Competing for the Future* (Cambridge: Harvard Business School Press, 1996); and Adrian J. Slywotzky and David J. Morrison, *The Profit Zone: How Strategic Business Design Will Lead You to Tomorrow's Profit* (New York: Times Books, 1998).

5. The classic work on transformational leadership is James MacGregor Burns, *Leadership* (New York: Harper & Row, 1978). See also his more recent book, *Transforming Leadership* (New York: Atlantic Monthly Press, 2003). For discussion more closely tied to the corporate setting, see Noel M. Tichy and Mary Anne DeVanna, *The Transformational Leader: The Key to Global Competitiveness* (New York: John Wiley & Sons, 1986).

6. Bruce A. Pasternack and James O'Toole, "Yellow-Light Leadership: How the World's Best Companies Manage Uncertainty," *Strategy and Business,* no. 27 (2002).

CHAPTER 7

FUTURE DIRECTIONS

NEW RULES FOR THE 21ST CENTURY

I never think of the future. It comes soon enough.

—*Albert Einstein*

THROUGHOUT HISTORY people have believed they were living in a period of unprecedented change. Change always feels greater to those living it. But today the word "change" does not begin to capture the degree of turbulence, the pace, or the magnitude of transformation around us. It is too simple, too calm a term. Given the amount of change, we can be sure that ten years from now some author will be saying something similar—and ten years after that and forever more. If one thing is certain, it is uncertainty. And the intervals between uncertain events are shortening. Everything is moving at a much faster rate, from many different sources, creating more unpredictability than ever.

In this sea of tumult, we are on the edge of a leadership crisis in both the public and the private sector. Institutions are too complex. Confidence in leaders has declined. The lack of integrity by a few has tainted the integrity of all. Temptations abound. Uncertainty is too great. If this is even remotely true today, what does that bode for the future? And from where will our needed leaders come?

This chapter turns to this challenge. Focusing on the three Truths is important for today's organization, and it will be even more so in the future. But within that context, there is more to do even for today's Top Companies. Before looking at these new directions—new rules for the 21st century—we'd like to provide some context about the ever-changing world in which we live.

SEVEN "GIVENS" ABOUT THE FUTURE

We travel the globe and oftentimes uncover stories that define our moment in history, that characterize the complexity and pace of work around us. Here are a few:

- On Thursday, September 13, 2001, just two days after the terrorist attack on New York's World Trade Center, managers at K-Mart noticed an increase in customer demand for American flags. The day before, managers at Target Stores had observed the same thing. Both companies attempted to purchase more flags from their suppliers. None were available. Anywhere. That's because on the afternoon of September 11, just hours after the attack, Wal-Mart noticed the same increase in customer demand and purchased every American flag, from every supplier, everywhere. They were able to do so because they update their inventory every seven minutes.
- If you have traveled to Tokyo recently, you've surely noticed unmanned kiosks on the streets, particularly near shopping districts. From the outside, these kiosks look like high-tech public restrooms, but on the inside, they are automated teller machines on steroids—they provide instant loans. Any Japan-

ese consumer with a driver's license can apply. Credit is checked, contracts signed, and loans are made in 30 minutes or less. The kiosks are owned by Lake, a Japanese finance firm acquired in the late 1990s by GE Capital, headquartered in Stamford, Connecticut.[1]

- In his book *The Future of Success,*[2] Robert Reich, the former U.S. secretary of labor, wrote about a company that has no factories or warehouses. In fact, it has no tangible assets. It builds generic computers according to customers' specifications. To place an order, customers call a toll-free number connected to FedEx's logistics services, which then passes the order on to a manufacturer that assembles the computer from parts shipped from suppliers all over the world. An invoice is sent from a bank that manages all billing and credit approvals as well as payments to all subcontractors, and assumes both the cost and risk of collecting from the customer. Customer service is handled by an outsourcing firm in Tampa, Florida. The company is really only a small number of people operating out of a single floor in Atlanta.
- We were gathering information for a client recently on the history and pace of computer technology. While it was amazing to review the unimpeded advance in computing power predicated nearly 40 years ago by Gordon Moore,[3] the future holds even greater, discontinuous change. IBM recently announced its intent to design a computer on a molecular scale—a computer that will literally float through the air.
- In the past year, nearly $12 billion of information technology (IT) and business-processing services were provided from India, the Philippines, and Eastern Europe. The pace of this work transfer will quicken in the near future. In the next 15 years, 3.3 million U.S. service jobs, along with $136 billion in wages, will move off-shore.

If you've traveled to Bangalore, India recently, you'll know what we mean. Nearly 200 of the *Fortune* 500 companies outsource their IT requirements to India. Many companies have shifted IT, accounting and finance, and customer service work to lower-cost markets. GE Capital, for instance, has 17,000 people in Mumbai, Hyderabad, and Delhi who process mortgage loans, insurance claims, payroll, and credit card transactions. British Airways Network Services, based in Mumbai, tracks the airline's frequent flyer miles. A telecomputing firm in Delhi pulls doctors' dictation from a toll-free number in the United States, transcribes the recording, and sends the text back to the health facility.[4] Ireland has more than 1,200 foreign companies employing well over 100,000 people. Intel, headquartered in Palo Alto, California, is Ireland's largest employer.

Today, these stories capture our attention and define our time. If you've ever worked in a large enterprise, you know the speed of a Wal-Mart is daunting. If you've held a mortgage for a home within the last 20 years, you know 30-minute loans are mindboggling. If you have lived long enough to watch the evolution of the computer age, you have come to expect regular, head-turning innovations. Even still, molecular computers get attention. Technological innovations once came along every generation, then every decade, and now in this nanosecond world, innovative breakthroughs are commonplace, more normative. And if you've discovered the representative calling about your mortgage payment is sitting in Mumbai, India, you know it really is a different world. Almost to the point that the very word "innovation" needs redefining. Indeed, we are not in Kansas anymore.

Industries that will alter our lives in the next 20 years, in all likelihood, have not yet formed. The power of technology and ideas, the confluence of both of these to build and to destroy with such strength and speed, means that the company that will dominate, that will be the largest in the world—the next Microsoft, IBM, Wal-Mart—does not yet exist, either.[5]

We are not trying to be alarmist, to use scare tactics to spur either action or, worse, paralysis. Rather, our intent is to be sure we focus on what's ahead, to the best of our knowledge, so we can better prepare ourselves and our organizations. No one knows what the future brings. But there are some events that are highly probable. These are the givens. We can debate how much, how fast, but in the end, the givens are hard to challenge. Below we discuss the seven givens in the context of leadership and talent. Once the givens are clearly established, we will turn to the New Rules for the future.

The Givens About Our Future

There is no shortage of futurists. Prognosticators provide us with plenty to think about. Geopolitics, germ warfare, genetics, biotechnology, the aging workforce, uncertainty, technology, complexity, ambiguity, stress in the workplace, talent wars, knowledge and income gaps, disparities between developed and underdeveloped nations—there is no end to the issues and challenges that lie ahead. They require a book all of their own. Instead, we've distilled these challenges and issues to the seven that pertain most directly to the topic of leadership.

The science fiction writer William Gibson once said, "The future is already here, it is just unevenly distributed." We think you'll find that true with the seven givens as well.

Speed and Uncertainty Will Prevail. Over the last several decades, the speed of computers has gone from milliseconds (thousandths of a second) to nanoseconds (billionths of a second). That speed is hard to fathom. Think of it this way: It is a compression of time that is the equivalent of a person's entire working life of, say, 2,000 hours per year for 40 years—80,000 hours—crunched into a mere 4.8 minutes.[6]

Speed is everywhere. Everything moves at a faster pace. Instant messaging. One-hour photo. One-hour laundry. Thirty-minute loans. Consumers can get what they want, when they want it, anywhere in the world. Providers of products and services are in great abundance in this globalized world. And they're readily available. The Internet makes them so.

According to Robert Reich, consumers today are more able to make a switch to a better deal than in the past. The easier it is for buyers to switch to a better deal, the harder it is for sellers to attract and keep them. Reich argues that the same logic holds for employee-employer relationships. Since it is increasingly easier for employees to switch to a better deal, employers must work harder to keep great talent.

While this switching heightens insecurity and uncertainty, it also fosters innovation. We are always working to attract and keep customers and employees. Today's innovations have a short shelf life. In the end, Reich humorously points out, "you will never reach a point where you can relax." Never.

In this sped-up world, preparing managers and employees for all possibilities is not doable. More than ever before, organizations that will thrive in this millennium will be those with clear values and beliefs that shape behavior and provide direction. They will be less reliant on hierarchy and approvals for decisions. They will focus on building the capability for employees at all levels to "do the right thing" regardless of circumstance. They will understand that leadership is not a position, it is behavior, and that the capacity for it is everywhere.

Technology Will Continue to Disrupt . . . and Enable. We live in a period of fast history. It took 35 years to get the telephone into 25 percent of U.S. homes. The television took 26 years, the radio 22 years, personal computers 16, and the Internet 7. And yet, just to show that the future *is* unevenly distributed, half of the world's population has never made a phone call.

It is an amazing time. Mercedes is experimenting with a new system that will connect the car's software via the Internet to a customer assistance center. This will enable them to diagnose problems while the car is still on the road and, in some cases, download the solution. Everything from elevator repairs; to restocking inventory, soda, and candy machines; to medical diagnoses can be done remotely and may not require a technician or an expert.

If you question how much things have changed, consider the following from Juan Enriquez in *As the Future Catches You:* The latest Super Bowl was covered with three-dimensional, 180-degree replay cameras. The game these days is so high-tech, you almost forget it's a game. But, if you can imagine this, you can't watch the 1967 Super Bowl since there's no complete film in existence.[7]

The laptop on which one of us banged out early drafts of this book—the other Luddite prefers pen and paper—delivers 100 times the performance of engineering workstations 20 years ago. And if Moore's Law—which holds that computing power will double every 18 months—continues to be true, then in less than ten years computers will have the processing power of the human brain and computers of today will seem like calculators.

Technology speeds things up, our first given. It fosters innovation everywhere. It forces the expansion of knowledge both individually and organizationally. Knowledge matters more and more, and managing and leading organizations and people in such a world is fundamentally different than in organizations of the past. Systems and channels need to be built to refresh, replenish, and retain knowledge. For innovation to flourish, collaboration—not authority—is the order of the day. Leaders will need to lead by influence, manage teams, and respect complementarities; directive, authoritative, and hierarchical managers are—and will continue to be—a dying breed.

Demographics Will Dictate Much of What Happens in Business. Throughout much of history, the average life expectancy was less than 18 years. People did not grow old, they died. Over the last 300 years, life expectancy has been rising, so much so that in developed nations it's approaching 80 years; and because of genetic research, our children are likely to be frolicking on the beach well into their 90s. But it's the decline of young people in developed economies that is a new phenomenon. By 2030, people over the age of 65 in Germany (the world's third largest economy), for instance, will make up more than half the adult population, compared with one-fifth now. At the same time, the population under the age of 35 will shrink about twice as fast as older populations will grow. The trend is the same in all the developed nations—the United States, Japan, Italy, France, Spain, Portugal, the United Kingdom, the Netherlands, Sweden—and many of the developing nations, like China.[8]

His eminence Peter Drucker wrote that "more than anything else—absent war or pestilence or any other unpredictable catastrophe—demographics is the most dominant factor in business today." But in this current economic downturn, the "war for talent" and the expected demographic crunch have fostered cynicism and complacency. Many companies today face excess capacity—they are shedding talent, not looking for it. Despite the current economic climate, we believe Drucker is right and that his words will continue to be even more true in the future.

In support of Drucker's proposition, here are a couple of points to consider. First, there will always be a war for *great* talent. With the declining population, companies will compete for significantly fewer people. Even in today's economic slump, top talent is in high demand. Many companies are churning their workforces, ridding themselves of modest performers and workers with skills and capabilities that are no longer needed and, at the same time, are looking to acquire talent for the future.

Even so, many leaders feel the anticipated shortage of workers described by Drucker and others will never materialize. Baby boomers will work longer, into their late 60s and 70s. Gaps will be filled by an increasing immigrant workforce. And the high cost of labor in developed nations will be more than offset by accelerating the movement of work to developing nations.

Clearly these trends are already under way. But Drucker's point still holds: The leader of today's large, modern enterprise presides over the most diverse workforce ever. And it will become more so. Facilities and employees will exist in locations as far and wide as Bratislava, Ukraine, Mumbai, Des Moines, and Chennai. The workforce will be more balanced in terms of age and gender. There may be more employees outside the home country than within it. Language and cultural barriers will be significant.

Leading is and will be a challenge. Understanding differences, the uniqueness of markets, and the communication hurdles and blending these cultural differences together into a powerful, competitive force—harmonizing this diversity—is a difficult task, to say the least. Finding great talent, building the infrastructure to do so, and overcoming the leaders' own cultural biases about what great talent looks like represent another hurdle some leaders will never overcome.

Loyalty Will Erode. This is not a matter of morals or character. It's simply a matter of the ease with which customers and employees can switch to a better deal, according to Reich. Buyers and investors can get better, faster, cheaper all the time from many places. Likewise, workers are able to learn about better opportunities more than ever and they enjoy relative freedom to switch employers without the loss of pension or other benefits that might have occurred in a bygone era.

When we discuss declining loyalty with audiences—of all the points we may make—this generates the most discussion and passion. Many people get upset that this is the state of things. We are not suggesting that employers or leaders not try to engender loyalty from their employees and their customers. To the contrary. But the reality is, it is harder and harder to do.

Work Will Be Done Anywhere, Anytime. In an economy based on knowledge, employees can work at their desk, in their homes, in a hotel, or on a plane. The concept of hoteling or working in virtual space is real. Eighty percent of Sun Microsystems employees work at home part of every week. One-third of the entire U.S. workforce works at home every day. And this trend will grow as technology allows. Employers will see their work and personal time merge. Weekdays and weekends will be devoted to activities in either realm. Employees will see the physical blending of their home and workspace as work and personal matters can be carried out in either place.

The leaders of tomorrow—even more so than today—will lead a workforce they rarely see. Spans of control will widen and will cross geographies and cultures. The "personal connection" that is so much a part of what great leaders do will be more challenging and taxing.

Employment, as We Know It, Will Disappear. Fewer and fewer people are "employees" as we've come to know the term in the last century—and, in the future, there will be fewer still. In 1952, two-thirds of senior executives reported they had been with the same company for more than 20 years. Today, job tenure in small businesses averages 4.4 years, and in large organizations, 8.5 years. More than 25 percent of the U.S. workforce is "contingent" and this segment is growing. In 20 years, that number could be 50 percent and that *could* be a global number. For many companies—particularly in high-tech—30 to 50 percent of the workforce is contingent: temporaries, part-timers, supplementals.

The Organization Will Become a Nexus of Treaties. The modern organizational form is about 120 years old. It's not likely to survive the next 25 years, according to Drucker.[9] Hierarchical organizations with multiple layers are too slow, cumbersome, and inflexible to successfully operate in today's world. For every layer of complexity, information and knowledge are cut in half.

In some ways, future organizations will mirror the Japanese *keiretsu*—a cluster of businesses around a core enterprise. Strategic alliances, joint ventures, and outsourcing create a web, a network that, at the same time, complicates and simplifies the modern enterprise.

In the 1990s, more than 60,000 strategic alliances were formed. About half of these alliances were joint ventures; the other half were nonequity deals like technology licensing agreements, research and development partnerships, or shared marketing arrangements. These will grow as companies try to extend their reach and minimize their risk.

Outsourcing is not a new phenomenon; it started as early as the late 1960s, but it is rapidly accelerating. Several factors are driving that trend. The emergence of the Internet and other communication technologies allows work to be done from almost anywhere, anytime. Cost pressures are forcing companies to rethink inefficient processes and shift work to outsourcing vendors in lower-cost labor markets. And, finally, the emergence of many quality providers makes it easier for fast followers to get on board. Despite the economic downturn, business-process outsourcing continues to show strong growth; it's expected to grow from $110 billion globally in 2002 to more than $173 billion in 2007, a 9.5 percent compounded annual growth rate.[10]

Leaders will need to forge and manage alliances, to build trust and integrity, and to reach agreement on shared interests and account-abilities. Not an easy task.

These are the givens. The future will be more challenging, faster paced. It will be more technologically complex, far more diverse in terms of both markets and the workforce. It will be increasingly dif-ficult to attract and retain our customers, clients, and employees. The organizations we lead will be more like confederations—loose clus-ters of providers, links in a chain—than today's organizations. Lead-ers face the challenge of fostering loyalty when they can no longer easily promise it in return.

On the other hand, the world does adapt. We are getting more prepared. Technology increasingly enables leaders to understand the complexity around them, to turn data into information about the people and markets they serve. Competitor moves and marketplace innovations—while many—are easier to monitor than in the past. Business schools and other leadership development institutions are catching up, changing curricula to match today's complexity and providing more real-time learning through the Internet. And while the world moves at a fast pace, we must remember, too, that we can often make adjustments faster than ever.

But when it comes to developing leaders, we may not have the luxury of time. It's difficult to speed up the processes of developing leadership capability. It simply takes time "to see how the whole thing works." It takes time to build the confidence needed to run complex, global businesses. It takes time to gain the variety of expe-riences necessary to lead.

Leadership will matter more than ever. And focusing on the three Truths will become more crucial as well. The involvement of CEOs and boards of directors will be essential; a rigorous and maniacal focus on talent, and the execution of the right programs, will be even more critical in the future. But within these broad themes, several areas require more attention even among the Top Companies. These are the New Rules.

THE NEW RULES FOR DEVELOPING LEADERSHIP CAPABILITIES

Rule #1: Develop a Seamless Talent and Business-Strategy Process

Many Top Companies have built systems that better integrate strategy, operations, and talent reviews. Clarity about strategy, the kinds of leaders needed, and specific decisions about how to build greater capability are increasingly the norm in Top Companies. But there's room for improvement.

Earlier, we made the point that the viability of the HR function rests on its ability to transform itself, to become more integral to the core of the business, much like supply chain, customer relationship management, and IT have done. As more and more transactional HR activity is outsourced or streamlined through technology, a core remains to provide "strategic value-added," as many reports on HR restructuring will say. But where, and how?

We believe the fusion of talent or human capital with business strategy and operational processes is the clear answer. Top Companies are leading the way, but more needs to be done to integrate decisions about people with strategic and operational decisions, to monitor and make the intangible value, tangible.

Today, we have the capability to understand the talent needed for a particular organization. We can predict with a high degree of accuracy who will succeed and who won't. We know and can measure the factors that lead to high performance and the impact of the leader. We can coach leader behavior for improvement. Talent-review processes, 360-degree data, and other assessment information allow leaders to make much more informed decisions about people and how to strengthen their talent. We can analyze the kinds of moves needed to develop capability and the sequence of those moves.

It's a start. But it's only a start. No company we know of has put it all together. HR professionals can lead and build the systems to understand and manage the intangibles. The line must drive it— must own it, as we've said repeatedly—but HR needs to step up and build it.

Rule #2: Do It Globally

In today's world, where you are doesn't matter very much. Work shifts around the global market as capacity and costs rise. An increasing number of companies will have more revenue and employees outside their home countries. But more often than not, a disproportionate percentage of leaders and high-potential talent is drawn from the home country. This will need to change.

The first step is understanding and clarifying what's needed from global leaders, then developing a global process to assess and calibrate talent from everywhere. That's the easy part. The toughest challenge is systematically moving that talent to build global capability. Global task forces, learning and development forums, short-term assignments, and being responsible for global businesses or functions are all part of the mix. But there is no substitute for being on the ground, holding a job, being accountable for managing a business, understanding a different market, and motivating employees from a different part of the world. It's expensive. It takes time. It involves risk. But if leaders are serious about building *global* capability, there is no choice.

Rule #3: Measure, Measure, Measure

It is here that many companies have a long way to go. Most companies—even at the top—are flying blind. We can see glimpses of what the future of measurement holds in Top Companies, but most would agree that what exists today is only a glimmer. We'd target several areas for focus:

- *Pipeline management.* Most companies track the number of candidates, talent sources, acceptance rates, turnover, high-potential pools, and so on. But even here, measures are often not *managed,* they're simply tracked. Information and data need to be turned into knowledge so more-informed decisions can be made.

  Few companies today have a handle on their bench strength. Many can produce depth charts or lists from acceleration pools, but few have been able to define the future capabilities needed and assess current leaders against these needs to really understand the true strength of the bench.

- *Predictive analysis.* Taking the lead from organizations like IBM, more companies will try to understand the roles and experiences leaders need to succeed, as well as the *sequence* of these experiences. This knowledge improves the efficiency of the leadership "factory," producing high-quality leaders more consistently.

- *Impact or results of leadership initiatives.* Organizations spend more than $20 billion on leadership development with little rigorous measurement of its impact and effectiveness. More longitudinal tracking of investment in leaders and their performance over time can help analyze the relative contributions of various programs and experiences.
- *Leader effectiveness.* In our 2003 Top Companies survey, only 45 percent of companies said they held leaders accountable for developing talent. With the proven influence of leaders on subordinates' career success, their efforts to improve their team's capabilities must be measured.

Rule #4: Use Enabling Technologies

When it comes to developing leadership capability, technology is significantly underutilized. Most companies' global databases of employees are only now being built—even among the Top Companies. The ability to find global talent and provide them with the skills and experience needed will be greatly enhanced through technology.

Succession-planning discussions will be dramatically improved. Bench strength will be more easily demonstrated, and what-if scenarios will allow decision makers to readily see the impact of various moves.

Leadership development and learning will be "on demand." Executives will be able to use the intranet and the Internet to find sources for learning and education when they want it. Personal "knowbots" will crawl the Web and provide information and knowledge tailored to an executive's personal development needs. Knowledge and information—learning—will be pushed, rather than pulled.

Many companies already have intranet sites that help leaders navigate internal and external courses and that provide online decisions and performance tools as well as access to internal and external service providers and experts. In the future, these will be more inclusive, provide greater accessibility, and allow simulations and testing before executives decide on a particular course of action. Users will also benefit from more mass-customization of learning and development to fit their specific needs. Internal and external experts will be on call, available for short bursts of advice, consulting in minutes—not in day-long trips requiring expensive and time-consuming travel.

Rule #5: Focus on Ethics, Values, and Integrity

Whenever we enter the economic market—whether for employment, to purchase a product, or to strike a business deal—we're confident that the terms of the transaction, the "promise," is exactly as it appears. We rely on the words and actions of others involved. What people say and do are moral and legal assurances to us that they are as they appear. We have trust that our laws and regulations protect us against illegal business practices, and we believe violators will be discovered quickly and dealt with appropriately. We're also comforted by the trust and integrity of leaders. We expect our leaders to have high integrity, to do what they say, and to operate within the bounds of the law. Such trust is essential for building organizational pride and the "above and beyond" behavior needed to compete. We have confidence that the commercial world operates this way. Without such confidence, the economy could never have evolved as it has.

But this confidence—or trust—is not always well placed, as the recent series of highly visible cases of corporate wrongdoing and malfeasance tells us.[10] In spite of this recent surge, the vast majority of executives and the organizations they lead are ethical and have high integrity. This trust and integrity take years to build but only moments to destroy. In a complex *global* world, we need to be ever-vigilant to protect this trust.

Trust and integrity have always been important foundations for leaders everywhere. Today, the value of trust and integrity is heightened. Organizations are less hierarchical and employees operate in relative autonomy, in global teams, with few rules to guide them. Spans are wider. Leaders may not see those they lead. The organization is a loose collection of partners, alliances, and outsource vendors. There may be a large contingent of part-time workers and temporaries, and a growing number of people passing through on their way to their next career.

In such a world, clarity about what leadership stands for is essential—the glue that holds loose pieces together. Leaders who can exemplify a steady state, a set of values and standards amidst the chaos, are more and more critical to the success and viability of the modern enterprise.

Many companies have developed guiding principles or corporate philosophies that serve as public statements of the organization's approach to business. They help guide and direct the actions of employees where rules and procedures don't exist.

Most important, these philosophies need to be living and breathing statements that embody how the organization and its leaders actually operate. They need to be derived from the values and beliefs of leaders, not from what is socially desirable. They have to help individuals decide what is right. Senior managers can exemplify their organizations' values through their decisions, and incentives can be provided for conduct that upholds these values. Seminars, training, and educational programs can be established to communicate the message of values and beliefs. But it's what executives do, not what they say, that matters most. And in this expansive, diverse confederacy, clarity around beliefs and values will matter more than ever.

Concentrating on the three Truths and focusing on the New Rules will create an important byproduct: a leadership culture, a brand that is unique and differentiating. It will become an important element of organizational identity, what the firm stands for around the world, and what its people embody in terms of quality, ethics, and values. It becomes the litmus test for who gets hired and promoted, and how decisions are made. The brand becomes a moral compass in a world of white space. No organization and no leadership team can afford not to be striving for this clarity.

The future can be viewed as an opportunity or a threat. We believe Top Companies see it as an opportunity. They are well on their way to building leaders. The future challenges are clear to them. They stumble. There are missteps for sure, but directionally they are truly leading the way.

IN SUM

The Gist of It

Focusing on the three Truths provides a strong foundation for building leaders, but Top Companies know that continued success means quickly adapting to a changing environment. Organizations will face seven trends in the next decade as they fight the talent wars:

1. Speed and uncertainty will prevail.
2. Technology will continue to disrupt and enable.
3. Demographics will dictate much of what happens in business.

(continued)

4. Loyalty will erode.
5. Work will be done anywhere, anytime.
6. Employment as we know it will disappear.
7. The organization will become a nexus of treaties.

Five New Rules will emerge for developing leadership capabilities:

1. Develop a seamless talent and business-strategy process.
2. Do it globally.
3. Measure, measure, measure.
4. Use enabling technologies.
5. Focus on ethics, values, and integrity.

Facts
- Work will continue to flow to those that can provide the greatest value for the dollar (or Euro, rupee, or złoty). Nearly $12 billion in information technology and outsourcing work was provided by India, the Philippines, and Eastern Europe last year; that figure will see an order-of-magnitude increase in the next 15 years.

- Globalization is a reality, and companies that grow global leaders will see a competitive advantage. Intel is the largest employer in Ireland (along with 1,200 other global companies).

Quote

"The future is already here. It's just unevenly distributed."

—*William Gibson, Author*

Consider
- What are the long-term trends in your industry, and how must that change your approach to building leaders?

(continued)

• What will your leaders need to compete successfully in a more global work environment?

• How will you manage the employment relationship with your leaders as the talent market becomes older, more diverse, and less interested in lifetime employment?

NOTES

1. See John Micklethwait and Adrian Wooldridge, *A Future Perfect: The Challenge and Promise of Globalization* (New York: Random House, 2003).

2. Robert B. Reich, *The Future of Success* (New York: Alfred A. Knopf, 2001).

3. Ibid.

4. See Thomas L. Friedman, *The Lexus and the Olive Tree* (New York: Anchor Books, 2000).

5. Juan Enriquez has written an excellent book that has inspired some of our thinking on the future. See *As the Future Catches You* (New York: Crown Business, 2001).

6. Alvin Toffler, *The Third Wave* (New York: Bantam Books, 1989).

7. Juan Enriquez, *As the Future Catches You* (New York: Grown Business, 2001).

8. Peter F. Drucker, *Managing in the Next Society* (New York: Truman Talley Books, 2002).

9. Ibid.

10. Gartner, "Business Process Outsourcing at the Crossroads," 7 January 2003.

11. For more on this see Robert P. Gandossy, *Bad Business: The OPM Scandal and the Seduction of the Establishment* (New York: Basic Books, 1985), and Robert P. Gandossy and Jeffrey Sonnenfeld, eds., *Leadership and Governance for the 21st Century (from the Inside Out)* (forthcoming).

Epilogue

We recall leaving one of the Top Companies after a day of interviews and focus groups with key leaders and high-potentials. It was snowing heavily on that January day and as we trudged to our snow-covered car, we felt a buzz of excitement. Interviews are tiring, and one might have expected the blizzard-like conditions to further sap our energy. But quite the opposite was true. We were energized by the energy we had just left behind. We couldn't stop talking about what we'd heard and the leaders we'd met. The adrenaline flowed as we retold the stories and experiences described to us, and recalled the intensity conveyed by those we met. As we brushed the deep snow off of our car, we wondered whether we'd be able to capture "it": whether we could discover the patterns of what they and others like them have been able to do—and whether we could help others achieve it, too.

It has been a quick but fascinating tour of the Top Companies, a peek into what they do to develop talent, to grow leaders. We learned that practices and single-pronged solutions are not the answer. There is no perfect way to develop leaders. There are, however, many options to consider, and each has its own flaws and variations, advantages and disadvantages. Focusing more holistically, the three Truths lead the way for practices and initiatives in the Top Companies. We believe we have captured on these pages what we experienced on that snowy January day. There is great leadership work going on in dozens of institutions. Leaders are working diligently every day to find and energize the talent around them. HR professionals are building strong systems and tools to provide more rigor and structure, to tie talent and business discussions more closely together.

We're also aware of the opposite: leaders who don't lead and who don't inspire. And worse, they don't know they don't. There is great talent in many companies working hard to be discovered, waiting for someone, somewhere to take them under their wing and, for many, it may never happen. Developing leaders in all too many places is a yearly program taught by university professors—probably inspiring in the moment but not the well-oiled system we see at Top Companies.

As we set out to write this book, our hope was to capture the attention of managers, leaders, and HR professionals who know that things could be better, who are aware that there is tremendous untapped potential in their organizations. If you've ever been on a strong team, ever been led by a real leader, you long to re-create that experience. Our aspiration was to break through the layer of cynicism that too many of us have, and be a catalyst for action for those who seek something better, more enduring, and more powerful.

As we look to the future, the challenges are daunting and the opportunities are great. Top Companies are well on their way to preparing themselves—and their people—to meet these challenges head-on. They're a step ahead of the rest and they're not complacent. No executive we met felt they had it nailed. None have checked "developing leaders" off their priority lists. That is yet one more differentiator for the best companies and the best leaders—they are less cynical, less complacent, always uncomfortable, and always aware that there's more work to be done.

APPENDIX A

TOP 20 COMPANIES FOR LEADERS LIST, 2002 AND 2003

2002	2003
1. IBM	1. IBM/Johnson & Johnson
2. Microsoft	
3. General Electric	3. General Electric
4. The Home Depot	4. Colgate-Palmolive
5. Dell Computer	5. Dell Computer
6. Federal Express	6. United Parcel Service
7. Pfizer	7. Medtronic
8. Colgate-Palmolive	8. Procter & Gamble
9. Philip Morris	9. PepsiCo
10. Johnson Controls	10. Southwest Airlines
11. BP	11. Whirlpool
12. Honeywell International	12. Microsoft
13. SYSCO	13. Cisco Systems
14. Centex	14. Wells Fargo
15. Intel	15. Federal Express
16. Citigroup	16. Pitney Bowes Inc.
17. Target	17. State Farm Insurance
18. Southwest Airlines	18. General Mills
19. Verizon Communications	19. Intel
20. Sun Microsystems	20. Merck & Co., Inc.

APPENDIX B

BUILDING A COMPANY OF GREAT LEADERS: A STARTER KIT

After reading the earlier stories about Top Companies like IBM, GE, and Colgate-Palmolive, you may feel confident that your practices are just as sound as theirs, if not better. Or you may feel completely alone in the leadership wilderness. In either case, this Toolkit will help you. Whether you're looking to "top off" your great practices, ensuring that they're truly 99th percentile, or if you need very straightforward guidance about where to start, you'll find specific strategies and guidance here.

We challenged the fundamental existence of best practices in Chapter 1, cautioning against blindly following the lead of companies that appear to have ideal leadership practices only to find that they aren't applicable to your company's strategy or market challenges. We reemphasize that caution now, having seen too many companies err in that direction. It frequently reminds us of the classic article "The Abilene Paradox,"[1] which describes a family's disappointing trip to Abilene, Kansas, that began under the mistaken impression that everyone in the family wanted to go there. It turns out that because of a series of miscommunications, Abilene wasn't a destination anyone was excited about. The story provides a simple but powerful lesson that's quite applicable to the process of building strong leaders: Before you begin building systems to grow leaders, make sure there's agreement among your executives on the desired destination. Do you really want a process that sweeps out the bottom 10 percent of your leaders each year? Do you really want to make leaders responsible for developing their own talent? Are you going to hold leaders accountable for the outcomes of leadership development processes? Be certain your current leaders understand what the destination looks like so they'll still be supportive when everyone gets there.

CREATING THE THREE FUNDAMENTAL TRUTHS IN YOUR COMPANY

We previously outlined and described the three fundamental Truths of leadership, using anecdotes from Top Companies like IBM, Honeywell, P&G, and others to illustrate how these Truths are achieved every day. Consistent with our objective to be very practical and actionable, we suggest action steps in this Toolkit to help your company achieve these Truths as well. We present actions you can take today to build strong leaders, as well as longer-term actions to build sustainable leadership processes.

This chapter is organized in the same order in which we presented the Truths:

- *Leadership Truth #1: CEOs and boards of directors provide leadership and inspiration.* Increasing the participation of your senior team, CEO, and board members in leadership processes.

- *Leadership Truth #2: A maniacal focus on the best talent.* Ensuring that high-potentials are carefully selected, developed, and rewarded.
- *Leadership Truth #3: The right programs, done right.* Choosing the programs and practices that are right for your organization and executing them effectively.

Leadership Truth #1: CEOs and Boards of Directors Provide Leadership and Inspiration

Increasing CEO Involvement

While some CEOs understand the importance of their involvement and the significance of their actions in building leaders, many others would benefit from some guidance on the topic.

As a line manager or HR professional, you can start moving your company's chief executive in the right direction with a few straight-forward steps. To give you fair warning, not every CEO is going to "get" this, despite your best efforts. There will be some CEOs and senior leaders who will simply refuse to admit that investing in growing leaders is worthwhile, who believe that the "cream will naturally rise to the top," or whose personal experience will overwhelm your ability to convince them to invest. Sometimes it's a matter of time. We've seen resistors turn to zealots time and time again. But if they don't get it after your best efforts and over time, assume they never will. Keep them informed of activities and do your best to neutralize them in meetings and budget discussions, but stop worrying about winning them to your side. Think of how many other people you can excite about this cause by expending the same amount of energy, and look for an environment that places greater value on leadership.

We describe below a variety of tactics for engaging the CEO and the board more fully in the process.

The Involved CEO and Board—Why They Don't Do It

With such a clear body of evidence that CEO involvement is critical to the success of building leaders, why do we still see infrequent, unfocused involvement from many CEOs? There could be lots of reasons. Some leaders genuinely don't care about the topic and there's nothing that can be done to change that. Many have unanswered questions about "how" and "why" and aren't willing to move forward until they're confident that investing the time, being visible and approachable, and modeling the behavior will yield benefits. Others might not know where to start. Still others may believe they're doing it when they're not.

Your challenge is to uncover those obstacles to taking action and build the business case for growing leaders. Many times, with a clear business case, compelling facts, and some promise of return on investment, you can at least get a foot in the door to try a program or two. Often it's just a matter of understanding what appeals to the CEO's decision-making style. We offer several suggestions:

- *Make the financial case.* How much more profitable would your company be if every leader performed at the level of your best leader? Identify the performance metrics of your best talent and your median talent, and do the calculations to show the increased revenues or earnings from raising the performance bar for everyone. If you have an aging workforce, chart how many new leaders you'll need to replace retirees in the next ten years and the cost of sourcing those leaders from the open market versus building them internally. Cite

Hewitt data showing that where CEOs are involved in growing leaders, their companies deliver superior results to shareholders. Or mention that almost all research on CEO succession shows that homegrown candidates perform best. Stress the need to have a process that fills all roles with "A" players.

- *Make the demographic case.* Two trends highlight the importance of investing in building leaders. The number of men and women who are "key-leader age" (34 to 45) is declining globally as the population ages, so fewer leaders will be available to select on the open market. The other trend is that quality of talent is becoming a hot topic, and many companies are raising the bar as they search for new leaders. The competition for this declining pool of top leaders is getting fierce, making investing in your own leaders even more compelling. Bottom line: You simply won't be able to buy leaders on the open market as easily as you did in the past, so start growing them today.

- *Make the emotional/values case.* Ideally, your company has a set of values, formal or informal, that describe how the company should be run. If these have been written down any time in the past ten years, they likely include at least one reference to the value of people in the workplace. If your company is truly going to live those values, shouldn't it be actively investing in building this great talent?

- *Make the competitive case.* It's relatively easy to get information from industry conferences, seminars, and books about what your competitors are doing to build their leaders. If you can find out what tactics and programs they're investing in, you can use this to position the investment you want to make as one that keeps you competitive in the marketplace.

We're such strong believers in this leadership Truth that the first question we ask potential leadership clients is "Does the CEO support this process?" If the answer is anything less than an enthusiastic "yes" and it seems likely that the client won't change his or her mind, we often won't take on the project. Without the CEO's support, the project will likely fail, diminish the role of HR in the company, and reflect poorly on our ability to help companies build leadership quality and depth.

We're hopeful that the new breed of CEOs, heralded by *Fortune* magazine as more "disciplined [and] deferential,"[2] will find the time to focus on building better leadership pipelines. Steve Reinemund at PepsiCo, A. G. Lafley at P&G, and David Cote at Honeywell seem to be able to find time for this, and it's tough to argue that they're in unchallenging business environments.

Here's a quick assessment to gauge whether your CEO is showing leadership and inspiration in growing leaders:

Does your CEO (do you) invest the time?

My CEO conducts (I conduct) comprehensive performance reviews at least twice each year with his/her (my) direct reports.	❑ Yes	❑ No
My CEO frequently meets (I frequently meet) with our high-potential leaders.	❑ Yes	❑ No
My CEO reviews (I review) our assessment of leader quality and depth or succession plan in detail, participating in action planning based on the findings.	❑ Yes	❑ No

Is your CEO (are you) visible and approachable?

My CEO meets (I meet) with many small groups of leaders each month to listen to their ideas and concerns.	☐ Yes	☐ No
My CEO communicates (I communicate) a company update at least once a quarter to all leaders through voice mail or e-mail, or in person.	☐ Yes	☐ No
My CEO encourages (I encourage) senior leaders to communicate directly with the CEO (with me), responding appropriately.	☐ Yes	☐ No

Does your CEO (do you) model the behaviors you want?

My CEO is (I am) an exemplary model of our corporate values and desired behaviors.	☐ Yes	☐ No
My CEO shares (I share) equally in the sacrifice required when cost reductions are needed.	☐ Yes	☐ No

If you can't answer *yes* to at least five of these eight questions, you need significantly more involvement from your CEO before your company can become a great company for leaders.

Getting the Board on Board

As we discussed in Chapter 2, an involved board emerged as a critical differentiator between companies that were merely good at growing leaders and those that were truly great. Board members who care about the quality and depth of talent in their organizations improve their decision-making capabilities around leadership and succession, but hopefully also have greater peace of mind about fulfilling the role of director. Given the small percentage of companies where board members are involved in building talent (only 31 percent of our 2003 Top Companies survey), most companies should have this on their leadership agendas.

Getting board members involved doesn't have to be complicated. If you remember the stories of boards at GE, P&G, The Home Depot, and others, their actions were very straightforward. We've identified five very practical ways for board members to become more involved in building great leaders:

1. *Make leadership a standing item on the board's agenda.* The best way to ensure that the board regularly discusses leadership issues is to make sure the topic is regularly on the board's agenda. Either quarterly or semiannually the agenda should include a leadership talent review, and at least once a year should include the results of the company's succession-planning process (see item 2). They can review the bios of five high-potential leaders they might not have met, hear about and approve the leadership strategy, critically listen to a presentation by a high-potential leader, or any number of other items.

2. *Succession-planning reviews.* In the interest of sound governance, the board should consider itself the steward of leadership talent in the organization and take this responsibility as seriously as any other. The hard-dollar investment in leadership salaries, perks, recruitment, and development each year in a large company can easily be a quarter *billion* dollars. The entire board should see a detailed report about the quality and depth of talent at the top three levels in the organization

(CEO, his/her direct reports, their direct reports) each year, indicating if these leaders' capabilities are aligned with what the company requires to successfully execute its strategy. In addition, there should be a detailed question-and-answer period with the chief HR officer and, ideally, identification of how the board will get better acquainted with the top leaders on the list. The process should not be left up to the "Compensation" or "Human Resources" committee—proper governance is the responsibility of the entire board.

3. *Location visits.* There's no better way to get to know the quality of the leaders than to look at the people and products/ services they lead. Like The Home Depot, P&G, and GE examples mentioned earlier, board members should rely on first-hand impressions of how the business is being managed. There's no substitute for the direct interaction of board members and leaders to get a clear sense of those leaders' capabilities and of how effectively they're managing the business. And, as in those three institutions, it should be a formal requirement of board membership, not merely a "nice to do."

4. *Personal interaction with high-potentials.* We heard an interesting example at one of our Top Companies about the level of board-member involvement in getting to know high-potential leaders. Each board member was assigned four or five high-potentials that they were required to get to know on both a personal and a professional basis. They needed to understand their thought processes, what they liked about the business, what they didn't like, how they saw their future there. In short, they had to get to know them well enough that, at the next board meeting, they could say they had a better understanding of the quality and depth of talent in their organization.

5. *Active involvement.* Nearly every company has an occasional

off-site meeting for their high-potential talent where a guru
or minor guru speaks, and where you hear from company officers about prospects for next year and engage in some variety of exercise about self-discovery as a leader. What's
frequently missing at these meetings is the voice of the board,
providing a shareholder representative's view of the world.
Similarly, you rarely hear stories about board members teaching in their company's leadership development programs, or
being as involved as the top team at Centex. This level of involvement, while perhaps not mandatory, provides a great example of good leadership and gives the board members
another opportunity to understand the quality and depth of
talent at the organization.

How involved is your board in building great leaders?

Our board of directors annually reviews the quality of leadership talent at least three levels into the company.	❑ Yes	❑ No
Our board of directors holds the CEO accountable for building leadership talent through his/her annual incentive.	❑ Yes	❑ No
Our board of directors visits our offices, factories, or stores on a regular basis.	❑ Yes	❑ No

As with CEO involvement, unless you can answer *yes* to two of
these three questions, your board is not contributing to leadership
development at your company.

Of the three leadership Truths, CEO and Board Inspiration

should actually be the easiest to achieve. We're merely talking about a handful of people committing to take individual, low- or no-cost action on a topic recognized as one of the most important of our time. No programs, no forms, no large-scale systems implementations—just deciding that this is something worth doing.

Leadership Truth #2: A Maniacal Focus on the Best Talent

The Top Companies rise above the rest through rigorous screening of talent and by providing challenging, uncomfortable assignments. "Rigor" involves clearly defining what comprises performance and potential; multiple rounds of assessment to ensure that no one is under- or overrated in the process; and frequent, informal performance reviews that allow for mid-course corrections if performance is above or below expectations.

Screening for the Best

The Top Companies are comfortable focusing extra attention on their best talent because they're confident that their high-potential identification process works. The actual steps they use to identify high-potential leaders are relatively simple. The process typically occurs during succession planning or talent reviews, typically once or twice each year. Line managers are accountable to manage the process; HR supports the process by facilitating the sessions, managing people data, and providing expert opinion. The fundamental steps in the screening process are as follows:

1. Separate performance and potential.   The best firms realize that a leader's current performance and his or her future potential for advancement are two fundamentally different measures (see Table B.1). Our 2003 survey showed that 63 percent of companies have some process for differentiating between these two measures. Before

Table B.1
Performance versus Potential

Performance	Potential
Defined	
Specific goals are set during the performance management process through standardized definitions across the organization	Through real-time manager conversations that describe the critical capabilities for future success.
Measured	
A combination of business metrics (widgets sold, budget made, etc.) and behavioral factors (develops strong talents, conveys clear vision, communicates effectively, etc.)	The manager's judgment, using a behavioral or competency model as a framework, and his or her knowledge of role requirements at various levels in the company
Who	
A leader's manager, possibly with input from peers, direct reports, and others using 360-degree or multirater feedback	A leader's manager, usually validated by others who have significant experience interacting with the leader
When	
Once or twice a year	Once a year for most leaders; revisited quarterly or semiannually for high-potential leaders
Time Period	
Past 6 months to 1 year	Next 0 to 3 years

anyone in your organization is assessed, make sure there are clear, agreed-upon definitions for both. Thoroughly explaining how to do this is beyond the scope of this book, but we can provide some guidance on each.

- *Performance* is typically defined during the regular performance management process and is frequently a combination of delivering business results (the "what") and exhibiting certain behaviors expected of leaders (the "how"). It's the typical scale on which leaders gauge their success in the organization. The time period evaluated is a historical one—usually the past year or six months. The definition of performance should flow directly from your performance management process. While this sounds simple, two very large challenges exist: the use of too many rating categories and an upward bias in the ratings.

    Too many ratings categories is a common design error— we've seen companies with six, eight, and even ten different levels of performance ratings in their system. This is normally the consequence of a good-hearted attempt to provide managers with foolproof tools to remove the bias from decision making. But the consequence is false precision—pretending you can be more accurate in differentiating than is actually possible.

    The objective should be to identify the best and the worst performers, both of which need special attention. Our advice is to use a three-category or four-category system, one that clearly differentiates who's excelling and who's failing. We understand the myriad challenges that simplifying to that extent entails, but we have found that the returns from the effort are substantial.

The other bias is *rating inflation*—an upward skewing of the average rating received and a consequence of the fear of defining anyone as below average. As a result, we've seen six-category rating systems where *everyone* received one of the three highest ratings. You can account for this in the calibration process we describe later, but it's much easier to simply start by accurately assessing leaders. It actually makes a very good case for the three-category system where almost everyone is rated average, and only a few are rated as superior performers or below average.

- *Potential* is a measure that adds a critically different dimension to assessing a leader. The time period for potential is the future. The potential of a leader refers to the ability of that leader to take on a position of greater responsibility within a specified period of time (see Table B.2). There are plenty of "potential" models available that purport to describe the 5,

Table B.2
Sample Definitions of "Potential"

"Ready Now": An executive with the versatility to fill a number of leadership roles in the organization. He or she would be difficult to replace due to the value he or she brings to the company.

"Expandable": An individual capable of contributing to the organization in a role with greater complexity, impact, scope, and scale than his or her current role.

"Appropriate": A person who is well suited for his or her current role and is unlikely to move to the next level or take on expanded responsibility within the next two years.

"Action Now": A person whose future potential with the organization is in jeopardy or who is fundamentally mismatched with the position.

10, 20, or more indicators that identify potential to advance in an organization. These models conveniently ignore the fact that the strategy, culture, and business environment of an organization may require fundamentally different future capabilities and make the definition of potential very unique to each organization. That's why we find potential is better defined by leaders' having honest discussions about the specific strengths of their direct reports rather than relying on static models.

2. Map your team.   Many organizations find that a Performance and Potential (PxP) Matrix (Figure B.1) can be a great tool for identifying their best leaders. A PxP matrix is a way of visually summarizing the capabilities of your leaders on both dimensions that allows easy discussion of their strengths and weaknesses. Let's say you're reviewing two mid-level leaders, considering whether either one should receive a developmental promotion. Leader A is technically excellent, holds many patents in your organization, and is popular with his teammates, although he prefers to work alone. Leader B has had ups and downs in her performance, but is seen as very bright and has successfully led a few teams through challenging times.

If you looked only at traditional measures of performance, Leader A might be rated as *Superior* and Leader B as *Average,* making it appear that A was a better candidate for advancement than B.

But if you discuss the potential of each leader, a more complete picture emerges. Leader A is very much a technician, interested in hands-on work to improve the core products of the organization. He likes working with a small team but can't stand the bureaucracy associated with "management," has difficulty communicating to nontechnical audiences, and isn't interested in relocating.

Leader B has always been willing to take on the most challenging

Figure B.1
Performance and Potential Matrix

| | | **Potential** | | |
	Action Now	Appropriate	Expandable	Ready
P Distinguished				
e				
r				
f Superior				
o				
r				
m				
a Average				
n				
c				
e Action Now				

assignments, which partially accounts for her hit-and-miss record of success. Even where she's failed, she's taken smart risks and significantly expanded her capabilities to lead teams. She builds relationships quickly and easily, has expressed a strong interest to "go anywhere" for the company, and thinks strategically about company issues.

If we map these two on a PxP matrix, they look like Figure B.2, with Leader B appearing more worthy of an investment in her future than she did before.

Now, using the PxP matrix, plot each of your direct reports on these two dimensions. You'll end up with something that looks like Figure B.3. This process should be done in a consistent manner

Figure B.2
Sample Partially Completed Performance and Potential Matrix

		Potential			
		Action Now	Appropriate	Expandable	Ready Now
P **e** **r** **f** **o** **r** **m** **a** **n** **c** **e**	Distinguished				
	Superior		Leader A		
	Average			Leader B	
	Action Now				

across the organization, and we've found that active involvement of the HR team can help drive this consistency.

3. Calibrate your ratings with reality. Both potential and performance are most accurately measured when the ratings are calibrated by other leaders who know the individual. By sharing their own knowledge of a leader's capabilities, other leaders in the organization can ensure measurement is being done as accurately as possible and that one individual's biases (positive or negative) don't overly influence the potential or performance rating.

The high-potential calibration process should take place in two conversations. The first conversation should be you and your

Figure B.3
Sample Completed Performance and Potential Matrix

		Potential			
		Action Now	Appropriate	Expandable	Ready
Performance	Distinguished	Smith			Dellums
	Superior		Jacobs	McBane	
	Average		Simpson Avery	Austin	
	Action Now	Jones			

manager discussing your team. Prior to this meeting, you should have assessed each of your team members' performance and potential based on the criteria that have been established at your organization.

The second calibration conversation should be with a group of your peers (likely those at a similar level within your function) to discuss their opinions of *your* team based on specific experiences they've had with them. Do they feel the leader shows potential for the same reasons that you do? Do they have a fundamentally different vision about what "potential" means for your department or organization? This is the time to get all those opinions on the table.

Your peers are also accountable to put their people "on the table" for your assessment and to have the same discussion. At the end of the day, you have a comprehensive map of the quality and depth of talent in your part of the organization.

Developmental Assignments: Maximizing the Gain

Our second leadership Truth is extremely powerful when effectively executed. Once you've identified the best, placing them in challenging, uncomfortable assignments with the right support engages the leader and helps drive high performance. The process is straightforward, but getting it right takes practice and dedication.

We discussed in Chapter 3 that developmental moves are defined by:

- challenging people early,
- identifying the right assignments,
- broadening experiences to see how the whole thing works, and
- living with your own mess.

Keep these maxims in the front of your mind as you plan, build, and execute your process for developmental assignments.

Planning the Developmental Assignment.   What Top Companies know is that with limited developmental jobs available for the many leaders, two things are critical: (1) assessing the strengths and weaknesses of each leader and (2) knowing which jobs offer which developmental experiences. Armed with both sets of facts, you can best match the person and the position. Top Companies have a strong process for each. Here's an overview of what each process looks like.

Assess the individual: Individual assessments should flow directly from the PxP exercise we just described. When finished with this assessment, you should have a very accurate perception of a leader's capabilities and weaknesses, which should provide clarity about the types of assignments that would be most valuable for development.

Assess the jobs: Different roles in your organization have very different developmental opportunities, and not just because of their unique functional characteristics. The general manager job in Malaysia might build very different capabilities than the general manager job in Belgium. Your goal should be to maximize the development of your highest-potential leaders by placing them in the job with the greatest mutual benefit for the business and the individual.

The senior leaders of your organization are likely to provide the best input on jobs, and they each should be interviewed to identify the key roles in their departments. Those key roles may include all of their direct reports, and it may not. It might even be helpful to look down a level or two to identify highly developmental roles buried a bit deeper in the organization. That executive interview, which can be done by HR or by a high-potential, can be as simple as asking three questions and taking very thorough notes:

1. What are the baseline capabilities that a leader needs to enter this role?
2. What are the most significant capabilities that leaders will build or learn in this role?
3. What are the potential derailers that can cause a leader in this role to fail?

Once those questions are answered, reduce the data to a summary that looks something like the chart in Figure B.4 and use this information when matching leaders and roles.

Matching Leaders and Jobs.   Once you've assessed the individuals and assessed the jobs, you have the raw material you need for the

Figure B.4

Sample Position Inventory

General Manager—United Kingdom	
Office Location: Birmingham	**Staff:** 12 direct, 850 in three factories
Baseline Capabilities: The U.K. GM role requires smaller country GM experience, with a solid level of functional expertise in finance, distribution, and regional marketing.	
Developmental Capabilities: This role offers the opportunity to learn about labor relations in Europe, lean manufacturing, multifactory management, and foreign exchange.	
Derailers: The workforce is highly diverse, drawing from the U.K. and Western and Eastern Europe. Culture sensitivity is a must. These plants have had significant union issues and require a highly visible, approachable leader.	
Languages: English; French or German helpful	**Average Duration:** 2.4 years

matching discussion. Top Companies are successful in this process because they can effectively match the individual development needs of each leader with the types of opportunities in the organization. This process typically occurs at executive or division staff meetings and follows this general outline:

- *Preparation.* The senior team should be sent a list of open and soon-to-be-open critical jobs in advance of the meeting. Consulting with their line managers, they should identify a list of potential candidates for these roles, which should be more than a list of the usual suspects.
- *Discussion.* During the meeting, each job should be presented and candidates for that job discussed. That discussion should include the relative level of each candidate's fit with the job and how it meets his or her developmental needs. You can vote, give one member of the team selection authority— whatever works best in your organization to reach the out-come of having the best talent in the best jobs.

No talent-hoarding: We suggest a "no excuses" standard be in place for these talent discussions. This means that leaders can't veto a candidate's movement because they see her as irreplaceable or there's not sufficient bench strength to replace her. At the Top Companies, a "no bench strength" complaint would likely reflect very poorly on the leader who made it. In many cases, the CEO "owns" your best talent, so they're not yours to hold onto anyway.

Leadership Truth #3: The Right Programs, Done Right

Organizations have many levers to reinforce the right behaviors and ensure they have the capabilities needed for success. They can hire and promote different leaders, and they can use performance management, rewards, communication, and engagement tactics to reinforce certain messages, values, and priorities. They can develop critical skills through assignments, coaching, and mentoring. Ideally, the practices in each of these areas reinforce the same set of behaviors and are well integrated (i.e., performance management seamlessly flows into succession planning).

Where to Start

The Leadership LifeCycle™ (LLC; see Figure B.5) that we introduced in Chapter 6 can be a helpful framework when building leadership processes. The LLC represents the major stages of a leader's life at an organization, and if each stage is managed ideally, all the levers you have to grow leaders will be working in concert.

Taking the first steps to grow great leaders requires that you understand what the ideal processes and practices would look like, where yours are today, and what your action plan is for closing that gap. We've oversimplified the action steps that follow, but we hope they begin to capture the essential steps you need to move forward.

Define. A company starting from scratch should first define what the ideal programs and practices would look like in each LifeCycle area, given what you've discovered about your leadership needs. If you're a fast-growing company in a changing environment, the ways you source, develop, and reward leaders are going to be very different than if your company has a relatively calm environment and a somewhat balanced business strategy (between growth and return). In a smaller firm, the vice president of HR might develop this ideal view of programs and practices him- or herself. In a larger firm, each functional specialist for compensation, development, and recruiting might create an ideal functional view of future programs, which can later be integrated at a team meeting or by the head of HR. As with the development of a competency list, the ideal future practices

Figure B.5
Leadership LifeCycle™

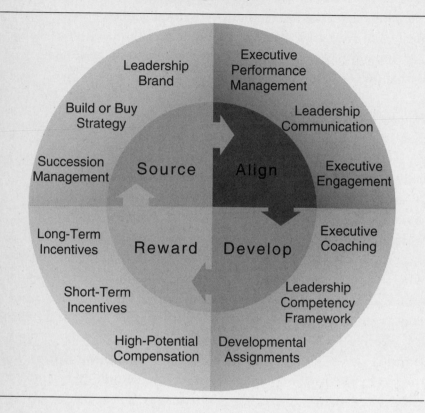

should focus on identifying the few, highest-leverage ones possible; it shouldn't be a laundry list.

Audit.   With this future view in place, conduct an audit of your current practices and capabilities. Since it's not always easy to get a clear perspective of a practice's effectiveness when you're close to the issue, this is an area where it's often helpful to get an external opinion. In addition, a knowledgeable consultant can both assess your current practices and bring to the table ideas and concepts that he or she seen succeed elsewhere. We've done audits that take four hours and audits that take four months—the time you spend depends on the degree of detail you want from the process. At the end of the day, the bare minimum you should have is an assessment of each LLC area comparing your ideal vision of the future with your current practices.

Design.   The next step is to design practices that work. Keep in mind our Chapter 4 guiding principles about how the Top Companies do this: lean design, coherence, innovation, and execution.

Some Tactical Support

Consistent with our message that the only "best practice" is the one that's best for your organization, we aren't going to recommend specific practices. But we are going to highlight two developmental practices that we heard consistently mentioned at our Top Companies—mentoring and coaching.

Mentoring.   There is a commitment to mentoring at the Top Companies, and the process is often mentioned as a key developmental activity. That's not surprising, since almost anyone who's been in a successful mentoring relationship will testify to its usefulness. Just to review, the concept of mentoring is that a wise individual develops a relationship with someone who can benefit from the guidance, and invests time to informally coach and serve as a confidant. There are a few great reasons that your company should actively consider mentoring as a key developmental tool:

1. *It's free (or at least very cheap).* While time has value, you don't need to get the CFO's approval to spend it. Mentoring can fit

into any schedule, no matter how busy. As at IBM and Colgate, putting a little structure around it enhances the process even more.

2. *It communicates value and key messages and allows assessment all in one step.* Mentoring is the "triple threat" of leader development tactics. In one series of conversations a mentor can communicate the formal and informal culture of the company, key messages about the company's direction, and how to negotiate its politics. On top of that, you get to see, as Lois Juliber of Colgate puts it, "if the kid's got it."

3. *It builds relationships.* While you can argue whether it's right or wrong, relationships are the currency of business—the more you have, the richer you are. There's no better way to get to know the influential decision makers (and have them get to know you) than through a mentoring relationship.

However, there is some disagreement as to whether the process works as well when formalized. One recent study found that the more formal the mentoring program is, the less effective it is. This research found that satisfaction with mentoring was lower in formal relationships than in informal ones.[3] That makes sense, since formal programs often match mentor to mentee by selecting mentors from Column A and matching them with mentees from Column B. With this mentoring version of an arranged marriage, it's understandable why it's much more difficult for the mentor and mentee to build natural affinity for one another.

Coaching. Before getting into how the Top Companies use coaching, it might be helpful to define the term, since many people use "coaching" and "mentoring" almost interchangeably. Coaching is the structured process of assessing an individual's strengths and weaknesses as a leader and then providing regular advice focused on *changing that behavior.* That's a key point to keep in mind about behavioral coaching. It has one goal and one goal only—to change behaviors. It's not about building technical capabilities, improving your public speaking skills, or improving your work-life balance (although any of those might happen when your behaviors change).

The coaching process should involve a formal assessment of behaviors you exhibit at work. This assessment can be based on your company's values, your competency model, or any other framework specific to your company. As we mentioned earlier, there is no "great leader" model that describes the ideal set of behaviors for any leader in any company. You need to assess your leaders against what really matters to *your* company.

Coaching has specific goals and, like any goal, should have metrics and due dates. Measurement should take place at the first assessment and with the same group of assessors at the end of the coaching assignment. The final measurement should assess progress against the weak areas identified originally—have they changed for the better or gotten worse?

A Model Coaching Process.   The inspiration for the coaching process we recommend here comes from Marshall Goldsmith, one of the best-known executive coaches in the world. This process is straightforward, focused on results, easily trainable, allows no excuses, and is completely measurable. In fact, our confidence in this process is so strong that we, like Marshall, accept payment for coaching only *after measurable behavioral change occurs.*

Our coaching process has sometimes been referred to as "Tough Love for Executives" because of its no-excuses approach. As Marshall says, "When you're over 50, blaming Mom and Dad is weak."[4]

The steps in an effective coaching process are straightforward.

1. *Assess.* Using a framework specific to your company, conduct an interview-based 360-degree assessment to formally define strengths and weaknesses.
2. *Gain commitment.* Provide feedback to the coachee and gain genuine commitment to change before continuing the process.
3. *Enroll the team.* The best coaches are the people closest to the leader—his or her peers, direct reports, and superiors. Coach them on how to coach the leader.
4. *Coach.* Regular monthly calls or visits to review progress and provide behavioral change suggestions.
5. *Measure.* Quarterly remeasurements of the leader's behavior to confirm change or flag issues that need more attention. Final measurement after a year or 18 months.

Each step is a powerful one if done correctly, and with the right effort and reinforcement, will result in lasting behavioral change.

To paraphrase Vince Lombardi's quote in our first chapter, building leaders is hard work, and it's work made more difficult by the confusing and often contradictory advice offered by leadership books, conferences, and consultants. We hope that this Toolkit, coupled with the examples provided throughout the book, bring some clarity to how Top Companies realize the three leadership Truths. We realize that there are many tools and processes available, some of which may be more appropriate for your organization than those we describe. That's part of the hard work—understanding what's right for *your* organization and not relying on any one source as the ultimate guide.

But while the precise route to great leadership might not be clear, the direction of the Top Companies appears promising. Their sustained ability to grow great leaders and deliver superior financial results provides strong evidence that this can be done. Their approaches are well within the reach of any company willing to dedi-cate the time and resources to make it happen. As are their business results.

NOTES

1. Jerry B. Harvey, "The Abilene Paradox: The Management of Agree-ment," in *Organizational Dynamics* (Summer 1974).

2. Patricia Sellers, "The New Breed," *Fortune,* 18 November 2002, p. 66.

3. B. R. Ragins and J. Cotton, "Monitor Functions and Outcomes: A Comparison of Men and Women in Formal and Informal Relationships," *Journal of Applied Psychology* 84 (1999): pp. 529–550.

4. Marshall Goldsmith, "Conversation: Behave Yourself," *Harvard Business Review,* October 2002.

INDEX

3M, 73
9/11, 5–6
80/20 rule, 107

"The Abilene Paradox," 183–184
Accomplishment Analysis, 88
Adkins, Rod, 93
   mentoring, 118
   selecting top talent and, 64–65, 66,
      69
Akers, John, 93
AlliedSignal, 88
   selecting top talent, 54–55
   time spent on development, 28
Alziari, Lucien, 42
Amazon.com, 141, 142
American Airlines, 34
American Association of Retired Per-
      sons, 82
American Express, 60
Anthrax threat, 34
Antoine, Dick, 76, 132
   board involvement and, 41
   selecting top talent and, 57
Arnold, Colleen, 75, 89, 93
As the Future Catches You, 163
Augustine, Norman, 27
   board involvement and, 41

Baby boomers, 4–6
Barrett, Craig, 116

Base pay, 153
Belief system, 115–119
Bench strength, 172
Boards of Directors. See Leadership
      development, Board of Director
      roles in
Bossidy, Larry, 25, 88, 108
   selecting top talent and, 54–55
   succession planning and, 116
   time spent on development, 27–28
Boughman, Jim, 135
Bower, Marvin, 60
BP, 181
British Airways Network Services,
      160
Bronczek, Dave, 33–35
Bryan, Lowell, 60
Burson-Marsteller, 6
Busch, Doug, 63
BusinessWeek, 2, 39

Calloway, Wayne, 101
Center for Creative Leadership, 87
Centex Corporation, 11, 23, 181, 192
   time spent on development, 28–30
CEOs. See Leadership development,
      CEO roles in
Charan, Ram, 43, 73
Chief Executive, 8–9
Cisco Systems, 181
Citibank, 134

Citigroup, 74, 181
CNN, 3
Coaching, 7–8, 152, 208–211
Colgate-Palmolive, 7, 19, 21, 25–26,
     132
  accessibility and, 33
  board involvement, 39–40
  building personal connections, 117
  communication practices, 120
  Human Resources Committee
     (CPHR), 86–90
  leadership programs/practices, 74,
     75, 86–90
  modeling and, 37
  risk taking, 123
  selecting top talent, 69
  social networks, 127
Collins, Jim, 49, 54
Communication, effective, 119–121,
     126
Compensation, 7–8
Conaty, Bill, 83–84, 88–89
Conger, Jay, 9
Cook, Ian:
  building personal connections, 117
  leadership programs/practices, 75, 86
Cook, Scott, 27
  board involvement and, 41
Cordiner, Ralph, 81, 134
Cote, David, 25
  CEO involvement, 188
  leadership programs/practices, 89,
     106
  modeling and, 37
  selecting top talent and, 62, 66, 69–
     70
  succession planning and, 116
  time spent on development, 30–31
CPHR. See Colgate-Palmolive, Hu-
     man Resources Committee

Critical capabilities, 137–138
Culture, 7–8, 115

Dartmouth, 74
Dell Computer, 21, 181
Dell, Michael, 73
Demographics, 164–165, 187
Donofrio, Nick, 65
Donovan, Dennis, 133–134
  growth strategy, 155
  leadership programs/practices, 78,
     84–86
Downshifting, 5–6
Drotter, Steve, 9
Drucker, Peter, 164–165, 167
DuPont, 39

Earnings before income and taxes
     (EBIT), 8
Eller, Tim, 30
Emory University, 73
Engagement. See Leadership develop-
     ment, Board of Director roles
     in; Leadership development,
     CEO roles in
Enrico, Roger, 132
  board involvement and, 43
  leadership programs/practices, 101–
     102
  time spent on development, 28
Enriquez, Juan, 163
Enron, 5–6
Executive Assessments, 88
Executive Check-Ins, 87–88, 108
Executive education, 7

FannieMae, 43
Federal Express, 13, 21, 159, 181
  accessibility and, 33–35
  FX TV, 34

leadership programs/practices, 89, 104

time spent on development, 31

Ford Motor Company, 82

Fortune, 28, 31, 57, 60, 160, 188

Fox News, 3

The Future of Success, 159

Gates, Bill, 55

General Electric (GE), 7, 15, 18, 21, 25, 132, 134–136, 181

  board involvement, 40

  Corporate Executive Manpower, 80

  digitalization, 83

  Executive Manpower Group, 88

  Internal Audit Group, 99

  leadership programs/practices, 74, 78–84, 86–87, 89, 90, 99, 103–106, 108

    · curriculum, 104–105

  modeling and, 35

  Quick Market Intelligence, 35

  selecting top talent, 52, 57

  Session C, 80–84, 109, 128, 135

  Six Sigma, 83, 106, 128, 140, 146

  social networks, 127–128

  succession planning and, 12, 116

  time spent on development, 27, 32

General Mills, 181

General Motors:

  leadership programs/practices, 73

  selecting top talent, 55

Gerstner, Lou, 1–3, 26, 133

  accessibility, 33

  communication practices, 120

  critical capabilities and, 138

  McKinsey and, 60

  leadership programs/practices, 91, 93, 96, 98

modeling and, 37–38

selecting top talent and, 54

succession planning and, 116

Gibson, William, 161, 176

Glass, David, 43

Global Baby Care, 36

Globalization, 170–171

Goldsmith, Marshall, 9, 18

Golub, Harvey, 60

Good to Great, 54

Grove, Andy:

  accessibility and, 33

  leadership programs/practices, 102–103

  succession planning and, 116

Harvard Business Review, 58

Harvard Business School, 73

Healey, Melanie, 103

  selecting top talent, 69

Henretta, Deb:

  modeling and, 35–36

  selecting top talent and, 57, 58, 69

Hewlett-Packard, 2

High Flyers, 60

Hirsch, Larry, 11, 23

  leadership programs/practices, 103

  time spent on development, 29–30

The Home Depot, 13–14, 15, 18, 132, 133–134, 181

  board involvement, 40, 41–42

  Business Leadership Program, 78

  Fast Track Manager Program, 79

  growth strategy, 155

  Internal Audit Group, 99–100, 108

  leadership programs/practices, 73, 74, 77–79, 84–87, 89–90, 99–100, 110

  modeling and, 35

  risk taking, 122

The Home Depot (*continued*)
  Store Leadership Program, 78
  Strategic Operating and Resource
      (SOAR), 74, 84–86, 109, 134
Honeywell, 18, 25, 181
  CEO involvement, 188
  group goals and, 118–119
  leadership programs/practices, 74,
      77, 88, 89, 106, 108
  Management Resource Review, 74
  modeling and, 37
  selecting top talent, 55–57, 62, 66,
      69–70
  succession planning and, 116
  time spent on development, 28, 30–
      31, 45
Human Resources in the 21st Century,
    18

IBM, 7, 16, 18, 21, 26, 132, 133, 181
  Accelerated Executive Leadership,
      104
  Advanced Leaders Series, 92
  building personal connections, 117–
      118
  communication practices, 120
  crisis, 1–3
  critical capabilities, 138
  Developmental Models, 108
  Executive Assistant Program, 92–93
  Executive Interviews, 89, 108
  The Firm and, 60
  group goals and, 118–119
  leadership programs/practices, 75,
      88–89, 91–93, 95–99, 104, 108
  mentoring, 118
  modeling and, 37–38
  new technologies, 159
  NextGens, 92–93
  personal digital assistant (PDA), 64

Pervasive Computing, 64
  predictive analysis and, 171
  reciprocity, 124–125
  risk taking, 122–123
  selecting top talent, 54, 57, 59, 62,
      64–67, 68, 69, 71
  Senior Leadership Group (SLG), 91–
      92
  succession planning and, 116
  ThinkPad, 64
  time spent on development, 31–32
Immelt, Jeff:
  leadership programs/practices, 82–
      83, 88–89
  succession planning and, 40, 116
  time spent on development, 27
Incentives:
  annual, 153
  long-term, 153
  vs. reciprocity, 124–126
Individual Development Plans, 86–
      87
Information technology (IT), 159–
      160
Intel:
  accessibility and, 33
  board involvement, 40
  leadership programs/practices, 102–
      103, 181
  selecting top talent, 63
  succession planning and, 116
Intuit, 41
IT. *See* Information technology

Job assignments, 7–8
Johnson, Bob, 118–119
Johnson, James, 43
Johnson & Johnson, 21, 181
  board involvement, 40
  selecting top talent, 57

Jordan, Michael H., 60, 62
Joy, Bob, 86, 120
Juliber, Lois, 19
    leadership programs/practices, 86–87
    social networks, 127

Kanter, Rosabeth Moss, 8, 73
Katzenbach, Jon, 8
    McKinsey and, 60
Kehoe, Michael, 68
    leadership programs/practices, 77
Keiretsu, 167
Kelleher, Herb:
    accessibility and, 33
    communication practices, 120
    succession planning and, 116
Kelly, John:
    group goals and, 118–119
    modeling and, 38
    reciprocity, 124–125
    selecting top talent and, 62, 65
Khurana, Rakesh, 9
Kimberly-Clark, 39
K-Mart, 142, 158
Knight Ridder, 39
Kohnstamm, Abby, 93
Korn/Ferry International, 38–39
Kreindler, Peter, 25, 45
    selecting top talent and, 56–57

Lafley, A. G., 132
    board involvement and, 41
    CEO involvement, 188
    leadership programs/practices and, 73, 89, 103
    modeling and, 36–37
    selecting top talent and, 54, 67–68
    time spent on development, 32
Lake, 159

Lawrie, Mike:
    leadership programs/practices, 93
    risk taking, 123
    selecting top talent and, 59, 65, 66, 67, 68–69, 71
    time spent on development, 31–32
Leadership development, 131–132, 154–155
    best practices, myth of, 10–12
    Board of Director roles in, 13–15, 25–27, 38–45, 184–193
    business context, establishing, 133–136
    CEO roles in, 13–15, 25–27, 38–45, 184–193
        being visible and approachable, 33–35
        investing time, 27–32
        modeling, 35–38
    critical capabilities, 137–138
    external vs. internal hires, 4–6
    fact-based guidance for, 6–7
    future directions for, 157–158, 175–177
        certainties about, 158–169
        global strategy, 170–171
        measurement, 171–172
        talent and business-strategy process, 169–170
        technology, 172–173
        trust and integrity, 173–175
    Leadership LifeCycle (LLC), 149–154, 205–207
    need assessment, 136–137
    on-the-job, 16
    programs, effective implementation of, 17–19, 73–76, 106–110, 185, 204–211
        challenging assignments, 93–100, 201–204

Leadership development (*continued*)
   high-potentials, identifying, 90–93
   leadership education, 100–106
   leadership pipeline, 76–80
   talent assessments, 80–90
  resources and, 20–21
  return vs. growth strategy, 140–142,
    145, 147
  selecting top talent, 15–17, 49–59,
    70–72, 185
   creating challenging experiences
    for, 59–68
   developmental assignments for,
    201–204
   results, 68–70
   screening, 193–201
  strategic leadership matrix (SLM),
    138–140, 143–144, 146, 148,
    149
  transactional vs. transformational
    change, 139, 142–148
Leadership LifeCycle (LLC). *See* Leadership development, Leadership
   LifeCycle
Leadership support, 7–8
Lifetime employment, 2
Livingston, J. Sterling, 58
Location visits, 191
Lombardi, Vince, 1
Loyalty, 165–166

MacDonald, Randy, 93
Magee, Rod, 30–31
Mark, Reuben:
  accessibility and, 33
  communication practices, 120
  leadership programs/practices, 89
McCall, Morgan, Jr., 60
McKinsey, James O., 60–63
McKinsey & Co., 60–63

McMahan, Larry, 31
Medtronic, 40, 181
Meija, Maria Fernanda, 25–26
  modeling and, 37
  risk taking, 123
Mentoring, 117–118, 207–208
Mercedes, 163
Merck & Co., Inc., 181
Michelson, Gertrude, 40
Microsoft, 21, 181
  selecting top talent, 55
Moore, Gordon, 159
  succession planning and, 116
Moore's Law, 163

Nardelli, Bob, 13–14, 132, 133–134
  leadership programs/practices, 78,
    84–86, 89, 103
  modeling and, 35
National Association of Corporate Directors, 39

Ohmae, Kenichi, 60
On-boarding, 16, 152
Orange, 42
O'Toole, Jim, 116
  transactional change and, 143
Outsourcing, 167–168
Oxford University, 74

PxP matrix. *See* Potential and Performance matrix
Palmisano, Sam, 3
  leadership programs/practices, 89, 93
  modeling and, 38
  succession planning and, 116
Parker, James, 116
Pepper, John:
  modeling and, 35
  selecting top talent and, 51–52

PepsiCo, 132, 181
  board involvement, 42
  CEO involvement, 188
  leader accountability in developing
    talent, 148
  leadership programs/practices, 101–
    102
  time spent on development, 28
Performance management, 7–8, 152
  selecting top talent and, 53
Peters, Susan, 79, 83–84, 90, 105,
    108
Peters, Tom, 73
  McKinsey and, 60
Pfeffer, Jeff, 8, 10
Pfister, Chuck, 99
Pfizer, 40, 181
Philip Morris, 181
Phillips Petroleum, 39
Pitney Bowes, Inc., 181
Potential and Performance (PxP) ma-
    trix, 197–201
Predictive analysis, 171
Procter & Gamble (P&G), 7, 15, 27,
    132, 181
  board involvement, 40–41
  CEO involvement, 188
  leadership programs/practices, 73,
    74, 76, 89, 103
  modeling and, 36–37
  selecting top talent, 51–52, 54, 57,
    59, 67–68, 69
  social networks, 126–127
  time spent on development, 32
"Pygmalion in Management," 58

R. J. R. Nabisco, 1
Rating inflation, 196
Reciprocity, fostering, 124–126
Reich, Robert, 159, 162, 166

Reinemund, Steve, 43, 132
  CEO involvement, 188
Return on Equity (ROE), 148
Riley, Donna, 92, 95–99
Risk taking, 122–124, 126
Roberts, Kevin, 103
ROE. See Return on Equity

Saatchi & Saatchi, 103
Sartain, Libby, 56
Senate and Banking Committee, 60
Service Quality Index (SQI), 34
Shanahan, Bill, 86
SLG. See IBM, Senior Leadership
    Group
SLM. See Strategic Leadership Matrix
Sloan, Alfred, 55
Smart, Bradford, 52
Smith, Fred, 13
  leadership programs/practices, 89
  time spent on development, 31
SOAR. See The Home Depot, Strate-
    gic Operating and Resource
Social networks, developing, 126–
    128
Soderquist, Don, 43
Sonnenfeld, Jeff, 4, 9, 39
  board involvement and, 43
Southwest Airlines, 3, 15, 181
  accessibility and, 33
  communication practices, 120
  selecting top talent, 56, 57
  succession planning and, 116
Speed, 161–162
SQI. See Service Quality Index
Stanford University, 10
State Farm Insurance, 181
Strategic Leadership Matrix (SLM),
    55, 138–140, 143–144, 146,
    148, 149, 151

Succession planning, 7, 11, 12, 18, 53, 116, 152, 172, 190–191
Sun Microsystems, 166, 181

Talent assessments, 18
Target Stores, 158, 181
Teruel, Javier:
　leadership programs/practices, 86
　modeling and, 37
　selecting top talent and, 69
Tichy, Noel, 32, 105
Tobias, Randall, 39
Tome, Carol, 85, 89–90, 99, 110
Top Companies for Leaders List, 181
Total return to shareholders (TRS), 14, 23
Trujillo, Sol, 42–43

U.S. Federal Aviation Administrator, 34
Ulrich, Dave, 8
Useem, Jerry, 43

Values, personal, 115–119
Verizon Communications, 181
Verschuren, Annette, 122

The Wall Street Journal, 3, 120
Wal-Mart Stores, Inc., 158
　board involvement, 43
　communication practices, 120

leadership development programs/practices, 78
　modeling and, 35
　return strategy, 141–142
Walton, Rob, 43
Walton, Sam:
　communication practices, 120
　modeling and, 35
The Washington Post, 2
Weidenkopf, Tom, 55–56
Welch, Jack, 7, 25, 134–135
　leadership programs/practices, 80–81, 103
　modeling and, 35
　social networks, 128
　succession planning and, 40, 116
　time spent on development, 27
Wells Fargo, 181
Westinghouse, 60, 62
Whirlpool, 181
Whitman, Meg, 27
　board involvement and, 41
Woolworth, 142
World Trade Center, 158
Wriston, Walter, 134–135

Yahoo!, 56
Yale University, 31
　Chief Executive Leadership Institute, 39
　School of Organization and Management, 4, 39